LIVING
FAITH

LIVING FAITH

Embracing God's Callings

KEITH GRABER MILLER

Foreword by
Valerie Weaver-Zercher

Cascadia
Publishing House
Telford, Pennsylvania

Cascadia Publishing House LLC orders, information, reprint permissions:
contact@cascadiapublishinghouse.com
1-215-723-9125
126 Klingerman Road, Telford PA 18969
www.CascadiaPublishingHouse.com

All Bible quotations are used by permission, all rights reserved and unless
otherwise noted are from *The New Revised Standard Version of the Bible*, copy-
right 1989, by the Division of Christian Education of the National Council
of the Churches of Christ in the USA.

Portions of this text were previously published in Keith Graber
Miller, "Transforming Vocation: A Mennonite Perspective," *Mennonite
Quarterly Review* 83:1 (Jan. 2009), 29-48.

Library of Congress Cataloguing-in-Publication Data
Graber Miller, Keith, 1959-
Living faith : embracing God's callings / by Keith Graber Miller ; foreword by Valerie Weaver-Zercher.
    p. cm.
Includes bibliographical references and index.
Summary: "Written from an Anabaptist perspective but relevant for
any denominational group, this book explains why the primary Christian calling is to be a follower of Jesus Christ and what this entails for vocational life" [summary]"--Provided by publisher.
ISBN 978-1-931038-94-2 (pbk. : alk. paper) -- ISBN 1-931038-94-5 (pbk. :
alk. paper)
1. Christian life. 2. Christian life--Anabaptist authors. 3. Vocation--
Christianity. I. Title.

BV4501.3.G685 2012
248.4'897--dc23

2012036487

18 17 16 15 14 13 12   10 9 8 7 6 5 4 3 2 1

To my children Niles, Mia, and Simon;
to my students over the last quarter-century;
and to all who seek to faithfully live out their callings

CONTENTS

FOREWORD

I could conceivably blame Keith Graber Miller for the fact that I am only now, on the eve of forty, figuring out my vocation. In 1995, having introduced me to the man who later became my husband, Keith conveniently failed to mention the thirteen-year age difference between us. Not far into our dating life, we discovered Keith's abbreviation of the truth and realized that, if we wanted to get married and have children, we ought to do so sooner rather than later. Otherwise, my husband liked to joke, he might be in Depends before the babies were out of diapers.

So it was that, two years into marriage and long before I had any idea what I wanted to be when I grew up, I found myself with a newborn, and then another, and then another. For a few years, my professional life meant writing a book review here and doing an editing job there, all the while grousing to friends that I had no vocation at all. Then, suddenly, our youngest was in kindergarten, and I had six hours a day to write and edit, and the epiphany broke over me one afternoon: this is exactly the work I want to be doing.

To blame Keith Graber Miller for my heretofore harum-scarum vocational life, however, I would have to use exactly the kind of narrow definition of "vocation" that he so eloquently undercuts in *Living Faith*. Vocation does not equate with paid work, Graber Miller tells us, and Christians who conflate the two risk missing the deeper pulsing of vocation that animates all of life. Graber Miller's capacious definition of vocation—as discipleship to Christ rather than career path—is good news for those of us whose working lives resemble a patched pair of overalls, held together less by sleek threads of professional advancement than fraying pieces of circumstance, caregiving, and part-time gigs.

Graber Miller's expansive notion of vocation is also good news for the woman who gave me change at the gas station and for my neighbor who is out of work. When vocation equals discipleship, it is available to all. When, on the other hand, vocation means profession, which requires education, which necessitates resources, it becomes owned by a relatively small elite. We do not need, Graber Miller writes, a "theology that simply and uncritically blesses the socio-economic trajectories of the majority of North American Mennonites." He commends to us discussions of vocation in the 1970s regarding the "perils of professionalism," as well as several streams of thought about vocational calling from biblical times and Anabaptist history.

Now that I am more clearly slotted into a profession, I am also glad for Graber Miller's warnings about the claims that our jobs make on us, the ways that we can be formed and de-formed by our work. We should have a "partial loyalty" to our jobs, Graber Miller writes, "a willingness to think critically about the demands of those roles." The capacity to follow one's passion into a particular field is a great blessing, and one the author celebrates. But *Living Faith* reminds us that the primary agenda of an Anabaptist vocation, whether or not it is lodged in one's remunerated work, is "to work at bringing healing and reconciliation in God's good and groaning world."

Ultimately, I have more to thank Keith Graber Miller for than introducing me to my husband. Now I can thank him for this book about vocation that I will give to my sons in a few years, when they are perhaps as confused as I once was about what to be when they grow up. I plan to re-read it with them.

—*Valerie Weaver-Zercher, Mechanicsburg, Pennsylvania, is is a writer and editor and member of Slate Hill Mennonite Church. She is author of* Thrill of the Chaste: The Allure of Amish Romance Novels *(Johns Hopkins University Press, 2013)*

INTRODUCTION

Just over sixty years ago, my spouse Ann's parents, Esther Rose Buckwalter and Ronald Graber, graduated from Goshen College—a Mennonite liberal arts college in northern Indiana—with high ideals inspired by their faculty and by their families. Among their parents, grandparents, aunts, uncles, and cousins were many missionaries, pastors, and church leaders as well as others who had asked thoughtfully throughout their lives, "What sort of life's work is God preparing us for?"

During summer 1952, just after their college graduation as they were planning for their August wedding, Ann's future dad wrote to her future mother, "We are going to walk down the aisle together and go out to try to make a difference!"[1] They were seeing their lives in God's context, understanding their lives to be directed toward making a difference in the world.

In addition to his family and college mentors, Ron had been among those who had been forever changed by his experiences just after World War II, when as a teenager he had encountered broken people and destroyed homes, schools, and public buildings. While still in high school, he had gone with Brethren Service Committee to Europe in August 1946, taking a three-week passage across the Atlantic on a boat filled with horses destined for those in Poland who had lost everything. It seemed a simple task, but it opened a window onto the world for Ron.

Ron returned from Poland, headed off to college and then medical school, and spent his professional life serving as a surgeon at a small Mennonite hospital in Aibonito, Puerto Rico. He had been influenced by faithful role models, had listened to those he had encountered in his life experiences, and had prepared himself for a life of service.

EXPERIENCING GOD'S GRACE

In my own life situation, two rather traumatic incidents shaped my early years and helped define my sense of self, my perception of God' grace, and my particular vocational and religious passions.

The first incident occurred when I was in an accident with my grandparents and other relatives. My great-grandmother was killed in the crash, and my grandfather and teen-aged uncle and his two cousins all were ejected from the car, with exotic combinations of broken legs and arms and ribs. Somewhere in the car's spinning I was catapulted through an open window and then over a fence and thirty feet farther out into a beanfield. Those on the scene first couldn't locate me until they heard me crying, and when they found me I had only three tiny scratches on my forehead.

Two years later I nearly drowned in a well on my aunt and uncle's back porch. As a three-year-old, I was curious about the round wooden cover on the porch floor, so I pushed it back and peered into the darkness it concealed . . . and then tumbled into six feet of water. I was drowning. Fortunately, lying on her belly, my aunt could just reach the tip of my middle finger as I stretched it out of the water.

In rural Kokomo, Indiana, it seemed everyone in my community knew about these incidents, so I grew up hearing the dramatic tellings and retellings of these narratives of my early life. I felt a little like the forehead-scarred Harry

Potter, who knew from early on his destiny. I know that hearing these stories repeatedly during my childhood and adolescence gave me a strong and passionate sense of purpose and a deep appreciation for God's goodness.

I now struggle with some of the theological assumptions (the God-assumptions) of that narrative, given the reality that not all children who fall in wells or who fly out of car windows live. But I know that those events gave me an early, embodied sense of a gracious, protecting God—I knew God's grace in my unbroken bones and air-filled lungs. Hearing about those brushes with death also gave me a commitment to serve that God who, I was certain, had saved me. By my early teen years my passion was clearly for some sort of ministry, broadly defined: I wanted to do something with my life that mattered, something that made a difference in extending God's reign.

SENSING OUR CALLINGS

I begin this book with these personal narratives because I'm aware that many young adults, or those of us who are middle-aged or older, could tell similar tales of the birth of our passions—a developing though perhaps less traumatically prompted inner sense of commitment to a people or a cause or to God, an unfolding sense of our gifts and skills (experienced both within and then also confirmed by others), and a gradual recognition of what we perceive as particular callings or passions.

I also suspect that some reading this book—perhaps many of us who are older—could tell considerably more painful stories of lives unfulfilled, aspirations unpursued, gifts unrecognized, callings unaffirmed, or vocations squelched.

For some of us the demands of life—of making a living, caring for aging parents or children, of tending to our or our companion's physical or mental health needs, of essential tasks that are part of running a household or living responsibly—squeeze out every ounce of energy we have. Sometimes the press of life reflects choices that are actual expressions of our callings, and sometimes those obligations distract us from our yearnings.

For younger readers, many of you haven't ventured far into any sort of life calling just yet. Nonetheless, you likely have wondered what you will do with your life, to what and whom you will be committed, where you will expend your primary life energies, what relationships you will form and lives you will touch, and perhaps what sort of volunteer or paid work you will do.

This book hopes to speak to those who already have experienced much of their lives as well as those who are younger, with most of life ahead. Ideally, this book could be used in intergenerational settings in congregations or small groups, with younger people asking questions and older mentors sharing stories and counsel. Or the book might be used by a youth group or young adult small group at a point of vocational discernment, trying to determine what next life steps may be, or how to deal with ethical tensions in the workplace. Older Christians may use the text to prompt their own reflection about life's meaning for them: how they made the decisions and commitments they did, what paths those choices took them down, and how they sense God's spirit in those movements of life.

Discipleship and Calling

This is a book about vocation and calling, and it is written from an Anabaptist perspective, or in an Anabaptist key, drawing on the rich resources of the forebears of today's Anabaptists: Mennonites, Amish, and Hutterites, as well as those in many emerging churches. Anabaptists were among the Reformers of the sixteenth century, occupying what some have called the "radical wing" of the European Reformation.

While Anabaptists drew from the rich history of their Catholic ancestors, they also agreed with many of the church reforms theologian Martin Luther and his companions were seeking to implement. In addition, they pushed for the clear separation of church and state, giving freedom to the church to determine its own policies and practices; argued for adult baptism, so that people could make a conscious, mature choice to be Christian; sought to practice peacemaking; and called believers to an active, lived discipleship.

In the train of those spiritual ancestors, I will be suggesting that the primary calling of all Christians is simply *to be followers of Jesus Christ.* To be "called" and to be "Christian" are essentially the same thing. To be called is to see all of the world, and to see our lives, through God's eyes, and to live faithfully as disciples of Jesus. That, to me, is what is most important about the notion of calling. In trying to discern our callings, we need to be able to say, in a way that matters, in a way that changes us and our perspective on the world, "I am a disciple of Jesus Christ."

To be motivated disciples, we need to discern our passions and link those up with the world's needs.[2]

When we speak of passions, we think of deep, stirring emotions; intense, driving forces; heartfelt yearnings. We think about being slaves to passion, about passionate pleas, or about sexual passions. We have passion fruit—the name comes from the cross-like seed pattern rather than the aphrodisiac nature of the fruit—and Passion Plays and Passion Week.

Passion has its Latin roots in a term that means suffering, hence the links to Jesus' final days of life. In its original form, passion also can mean being acted upon, having some genetic or nurtured-in drives or longings that compel us toward something.

I've always loved the concept of passion in its many forms. One of the great pleasures of teaching at the college level is being able to observe the passion of college students—passion for causes, passion for justice, passion for learning, passion in new relationships. I'm a big fan of passion; my sense is that even misdirected passion is better than no passion of all.

Passions can be problematic, of course. Some passions cannot or should not be fulfilled. But more often than not, passion is life-giving, empowering, and energizing. Passion inspires those who witness it in others. It opens us to embracing the mundane, and to seeking that which seems beyond our reach.

Not surprisingly, many of our passions are directly related to the ways in which we spend much of our lives—parenting, teaching, managing, healing, studying, hosting, creating, constructing, caretaking. Other passions get squeezed between the cracks of our lives—what we sometimes refer to as hobbies or avocations.

As long as we're breathing, as long as can make choices, we are still able to redirect our attentions and our energies and our being to our passions. When assigning papers for my classes, I always tell students to only write on topics or questions they actually care about, something that inspires or motivates them or sucks them in. Life is far too short to research and write papers simply because they are assigned. Once during a guest lecture on our campus, a retired faculty member got up and left before the end of the rather redundant and uninsightful presentation. I later asked why she had left, and she said, "Life's too short to sit through this sort of nonsense."

I believe God gives those who commit themselves to Christian faith the holy longing to be disciples of Christ. God also gifts each of us with particular abilities, abilities that can be used in God's service in the world.

WHERE THIS JOURNEY WILL TAKE US

In the first four chapters of this book, we will be examining how vocation or calling have been understood in the Christian tradition: in overall Christian history, with an initial explanation of Anabaptist concerns (Chapter 1); in the biblical context (Chapter 2); for Martin Luther, John Calvin, and other Reformers (Chapter 3); and for the sixteenth-century Anabaptists (Chapter 4).

The next several chapters of the book allow us to address the actual "work" of Anabaptists over the last several centuries (Chapter 5); how Mennonite churches have shifted in their blessings of expanded particular callings (Chapter 6); and historical and contemporary Mennonite perspectives on callings to ministry (Chapter 7).

The final two chapters of the book (Chapter 8 and Chapter 9) offer six vocational guidelines for those seeking to be faithful disciples of Jesus Christ.

Each chapter concludes with questions to stimulate discussions in class or small-group settings, with the hope that much of our vocational learning will come from hearing each others' counsel and stories.

I am grateful to many people for their assistance in the production of this book: to multiple student assistants over the last decade who assisted with my initial research: Nicole Olivia Cober Bauman, Krista Showalter Ehst, Luke Kreider, and Breanna Nickel; to Jeffrey Moore, my research assistant, who meticulously prepared the index; to Mary Lehman Yoder, Albert J. Meyer, J. R. Burkholder, David Schrock-Shenk, Michael G. Cartwright, Paul Keim, and Bob Yoder, who read earlier drafts of the text; to Becky Bontrager Horst, who encouraged me to write and research this text and provided funding through Lilly Endowment monies provided to Goshen College's Cultivating Authentic Leaders for Life (CALL) program; to Michael A. King, with whom I have worked on several books and for whom I have great editorial appreciation; and to my colleagues and students, whose perspectives always have enriched my reflection.

AN INVOCATION

When discussing many aspects of Christian life, including vocation, it is often good to begin with invocation. In the process of researching and writing this book, a particular statement of faith has taken on new meaning for me. The reading is from the worship resources at the back of

Hymnal: A Worship Book, a Mennonite and Church of the Brethren hymnal, and says in abbreviated fashion much of what I hope to say in this study text. It is with this confession that we begin:

> I believe God has made us God's people,
> To invite others to follow Christ,
> To encourage one another to deeper commitment,
> To proclaim forgiveness of sins and hope,
> To reconcile all people to God through word and deed,
> To bear witness to the power of love over hate,
> To meet the daily tasks of life with purpose,
> To work for justice where there is oppression,
> To suffer joyfully for the cause of right,
> To the ends of the earth,
> To the end of the age
> To the praise of God's glory. Amen.

QUESTIONS FOR REFLECTION

1. What is your own vocational story, and how does it support or critique what the author is saying in this Introduction?

2. What previous associations have you had with the concept of vocation or calling? What do you know about the concept in your own faith tradition?

3. How might reflecting on vocation be different for someone in high school, as opposed to someone in her seventies or eighties?

4. Is passion a God-given good? What sorts of passions seem to reflect God's desires for Christian believers? What sorts of passions might be problematic?

5. What are your deep yearnings?

6. What would you add to the statement of faith above, to make it better reflect your own convictions and commitments?

LIVING FAITH

Chapter 1

FINDING OUR WAY

In David Guterson's epic novel *East of the Mountains*,[1] physician Ben Givens is in the later stages of colon cancer. While traveling, the doctor reminisces about the decisions and commitments he has made throughout his life. Ben's mother had herself died too early of pancreatic cancer. In his reflections, Ben recalls a conversation with his mother one evening some months before her own death in the mid-1930s.

After working in the family's apple orchards all day, Ben had offered to help his mother cook the evening meal or clear the ditches, but his mother had insisted that he read instead. She said he needed to be prepared for that eventual day when he would leave the family orchards, doing "whatever is in the spirit of who you are. . . . Whatever God plans for you."

Once, after their pastor had preached on Adam and Eve being thrust from the garden and compelled to work, Givens says his mother had revised the sermon for him and his brothers on the way home from church. A lifetime Presbyterian, she offered her own interpretation of the Westminster Shorter Catechism, arguing that "work was an expression of love for God," the avenue by which we could know God. Drawing on her knowledge of theologian John Calvin's view of vocation, she said our lives are "full of worthy tasks to accomplish in accordance with our particular design, in such a way that we are lifted up, to ascend by the work God means for us to do, toward a higher love of [God]." Ben says his mother insisted that it is through the work we do that we know ourselves.[4]

Many of us may recall similar conversations with our parents or mentors, although those conversations may not have included references to John Calvin or the Westminster Shorter Catechism. Presbyterians and others who emerge from the Reformed tradition of Ulrich Zwingli and Calvin, and Lutherans in the train of the great Reformer Martin Luther, have developed rather full and formal visions of the concept of vocation, as we will see in the next chapter.

DISCERNING A VOCATION

One of the most foundational periods for my own vocational discernment came during my sophomore year of college, when I lived about five years of life in one eight-month block, a period filled with both tragedy and joy. The turbulence began when I left for a six-week backpacking tour of Europe, my first extended spell away from home.

While in Italy I got a glimpse of Christian faith in the early centuries, a high-octane Christianity that indelibly etched people's lives. I prayed in the underground catacombs outside Rome where early Christians met in secret, fearing for their lives but desperate to worship nonetheless, and I saw the Roman coliseum where our faith ancestors suffered for their convictions. It was tremendously moving to visit these sacred and terrible sites.

The month after my return to the States, in early March, I experienced a lung collapse—a pneumothorax—and found myself hospitalized for several days and in bed for a number more. It was a strange illness, probably related to a congenital defect in my lungs.

Later that spring I experienced sophomore uncertainty, a disease that sometimes strikes college students. I was asking all sorts of vocational questions, uncertain of what I wanted to do with my life. Should I continue with school if I had no idea what I was going to be when I grew up? I returned home in May and began working for my brother-in-law and his family in their construction business. Not long after I began doing carpentry, my sister left her husband, with whom I was working. That made my ongoing employment awkward, though I stuck with it throughout the summer and fall.

I know that I am now a college professor partly because through working in construction I recognized that—unlike Jesus—I have almost no carpentry skills. Failure in that arena drove me back to school, where I had been more successful and had experienced much energy and joy.

Out of the crucible of that year, the intellectual and emotional and physical and spiritual wrenching of my being, I made a forward commitment of faith, an adult decision to follow in the way of Christ. I had been baptized much earlier, at age twelve, in what I've sometimes described as my "breech birth" into the reign of God: scared rear-first into God's reign. At that pre-adolescent point I had only been frightened of death and post-death destiny—my same-age cousin had died tragically the previous year—and so I had made a faith commitment to save myself *from* something. Now I was making a commitment to be saved *for* something.

At the same time I began to sense more clearly a calling to and desire for ministry of some sort, whether in pastoring or writing or teaching or whatever, a commitment that continues for me. I knew that my life's work had to be in service of Christ and the church. Construction can be in the service of Christ and the church, too, of course, as can be accounting, art, owning a business, working in a factory, being in the health care field, or nearly any other role.

For me, I realized that for the development of my own gifts—which did not involve working with my hands—I would need to complete my formal education, so I returned to college and completed my undergraduate degree.

After school, when a job fell in my lap, I began working as a journalist, editing and writing for two newspapers over the next two years, believing journalism was a worthy profession but also knowing my life would likely yet take some other turns.

A few years later I became a co-pastor in my home congregation when a vacancy opened and the congregation tapped me on the shoulder and encouraged me to study alongside half-time pastoral work. I began an elongated, five-year program at Associated Mennonite Biblical Seminary in Elkhart, Indiana.

After nearly four years pastoring at that church, I became interim campus minister at Goshen College, and then eventually, after completing my doctoral degree, moved into teaching in the Bible and Religion department at Goshen.

It is clear to me now, looking back, that each of these specific work settings prepared me for the next vocational stage, that they wove themselves into a kind of tapestry of a life. Each stage contributed to the following one, allowing me to test and hone certain skills that I still use today in what genuinely feels like the place where I should be, the place where God has called me to serve as a disciple of Christ.

ANABAPTIST CONCERNS ABOUT VOCATION

The personal story I just told is similar to what sixteenth-century reformers were discovering. Vocation in its classic Protestant form is much more expansive than an occupation, profession, or paid work. All social relations—family commitments and friendships, extracurricular involvements, participation in the life of communities—are understood as places "into which God calls us to serve God and neighbor."[5] From a Protestant view these are not "avocations," things one does beyond paid work, but part of one's vocation.

Nonetheless, Anabaptists have had a rather tortured history with the notion of vocation or calling. We certainly didn't invent the concept, nor did we even embrace it when other reformers began their innovative explorations of the centuries-old idea.

At least three factors, all of which we will examine in later chapters, have made it difficult for Mennonites and other Anabaptists to talk about vocation. First, in Europe and elsewhere where Mennonites emerged or emigrated, some crafts and professions were prohibited for Mennonites. Pacifist Anabaptists, with their radical teachings about discipleship and economics, simply were not allowed to engage in certain societal roles.

Second, for theological and ethical reasons, Mennonites have sometimes chosen not to participate in some economic and governmental activities and roles, whether or not they would have been available to them. Luther and Calvin had expanded Christians' view of where God's creative and redeeming activities could take place—far beyond the monastery, to say the least! While Anabaptists were grateful for that expansion, they were less willing to bless nearly all forms of work and all social responsibilities. They were troubled by the fusion of God's will and calling with existing political systems and economic structures.

And, finally, a certain level of uncertainty about the role of pastors and priests characterized early and later Anabaptists. That anticlericalism was a response to corrupt or unfaithful leadership models they could observe around them as well as the martyrdom of many gifted leaders in the early decades of Anabaptism.

Together these three historical factors—prohibition from participating in some societal roles, choosing not to engage in some professions for ethical reasons, and uncertainty about officially designated church leaders—make talking about vocation difficult for Mennonites, whether the conversation is about the more general sense of seeing God's hand in our work-a-day worlds or more specifically addressing pastoral vocation.

Contemporary Anabaptists should reflect carefully on their spiritual ancestors' perspectives on vocation. We need to assess, critically and thoughtfully, what it has meant from within our own theological tradition to discern God's callings in and on our lives. Only then can we work toward a faithful, authentic, Anabaptist perspective on vocation. We begin in Chapter 2 by addressing the ways in which understandings of God-blessed work developed in the Bible and in the early Christian centuries, and then in Chapter 3 the manners in which Protestant Reformers, including Anabaptists, transformed those views of "divine" or "religious" work.

QUESTIONS FOR REFLECTION

1. Do you identify in any way with Ben Givens, the character in the *East of the Mountains* novel? Or with his mother? In what way?

2. If you are older, do you identify with the author's sense of God weaving together a "tapestry of life," even when we don't plan or arrange for it? If you are younger, can you imagine your life in the beginning stages of that artistic formation?

3. What early work experiences have affected your own discernment about what work you may do in life, or what work you have done?

4. Would you agree with some church leaders that all social relations—places where we interact with others—are places "into which God calls us to serve God and neighbor"?

5. What springs to mind when you hear the terms *divine* or *religious* work? How might your own work, or the work you may do someday, fit these categories?

6. If you have made a commitment of faith and Christian discipleship, what did that commitment mean to you at

the time it occurred? What does it mean to you now? How does that commitment relate to the work you may do in life, or the work you have done?

Chapter 2

HEARING THE CALL

The story is told of a middle-aged man informing his elderly mother about a friend who had died too young—in her mid-fifties. She had left behind her adult children and a number of grandchildren who had come to depend on her. The man's elderly mother said, "Why couldn't it have been me? I am ninety-three years old, and she was so young. I've worked hard all my life to serve the Lord, and I'm ready to go."

"Now Mother," said the son, "the Lord has left you here on earth for a purpose. God must have something else for you to do."

"Well, I'm telling you right now," she quickly snapped, "I'm not gonna do it."

The woman in this imaginary story might have good biblical company. By the time Moses heard God's call out of the flaming shrubbery (Exod. 3), he was a burned-out fugitive, on the run. He had fled from the pharaoh, leaving behind his people, who were slaves in Egypt. So when God's Word came to Moses, he was out tending his father-in-law Jethro's flocks, a job that would prepare Moses for the task to which he was to devote himself, the task of shepherding God's flock out of Egypt.

Some observers have suggested that the burning bush

was not a miracle: it was a test. God wanted to find out whether or not Moses could pay attention to something for more than a few minutes. When Moses did, God spoke.

God said, "I've heard the cry of my people, observed their misery, and I'm calling on you to go to free them. I will send you to Pharaoh to bring my people, the Israelites, out of Egypt."

What we remember about the story is that after God called Moses he went back to Egypt, confronted the pharaoh, and led the Hebrew people through the Red Sea and into the Promised Land. And that is true enough. But we usually overlook the conversation between Moses and God. Moses could hear God well enough, and he knew what God was asking of him. But he needed a bit of a shove to open himself to that calling.

God appears dramatically before Moses and says, "I am the God of your ancestors, the God of Abraham and Sarah, the God of Isaac and Rebekah, the God of Jacob and Rachel and Leah." And then after God notes the people are crying out and tells Moses rather directly that he is being sent to bring the Israelites out of Egypt, Moses says, "Okay, sounds good to me."

Not quite. Moses immediately says to God, "Who am I that I should go to Pharaoh, and bring the Israelites out of Egypt?" So God says, "I will be with you," and gives Moses the sign that the people will worship God on this mountain after they are freed from slavery. And then Moses says, "Okay, sounds good to me"?

No, Moses says to God, "If I come to the Israelites and say to them, 'The God of your ancestors has sent me to you,' and they ask me, 'what is his name?' what shall I say to them?" God retorts, a little exasperated already, "I am who I am." And then God tells Moses to assemble the elders of Israel and tell them what God is doing for them. "They will listen to your voice," says God.

And then Moses says, "Okay, sounds good to me"?

Wrong again. This time Moses says, "But suppose they do not believe me or listen to me, but say, 'The Lord did not appear to you.'" So God does a couple of miracles with a staff that turns into a snake and then back into a staff, and with Moses' hand turning leprous and then being restored.

So then Moses says, "Okay, sounds good to me"?

Moses still hasn't fully grasped his calling. He says instead, "O my Lord, I have never been eloquent, neither in the past nor even now that you have spoken to your servant; but I am slow of speech and slow of tongue."

God says, "Look, I'm the one who gives speech to mortals. Now go, and I will be with your mouth and teach you what to speak."

And now Moses says, "Okay, sounds good to me"?

No. This is actually a rather remarkable story. Moses says instead, "O my Lord, please send someone else."

It took six rounds with God, five excuses, with a helper thrown in, before Moses finally agreed to accept his calling. Moses nearly dropped off the face of holy history. What eventually happens, of course, is that Moses' brother Aaron goes with him, and Aaron, the more articulate one, speaks for Moses. God speaks through both Moses and Aaron, and as they speak these words to the Israelites, "The people believed; and when they heard that the Lord had given heed to the Israelites and that he had seen their misery, they bowed down and worshipped" (Exod. 4:31).

BIBLICAL CALLINGS

Both the Old Testament and the New Testament—or Hebrew Scriptures and Christian Scriptures, as we often say today—are thick with similar stories of calling, beginning with God's calling of Abram and Sarai in Genesis 12. But even before that we have the concept of calling, sometimes coupled with the Hebrew word for "name" as Adam and Eve "call by name" the creatures.

Later in Hebrew Scriptures we hear of God's call to the stubborn Moses in Exodus 3, as already described above, Gideon's call through an angel of the Lord in Judges 6, Samuel's call as a child in 1 Samuel 3, the prophetic calling of Isaiah (Isa. 6), Ezekiel's dramatic, open-heaven vision of God (Ezek. 1), and Jeremiah's call and response (Jer. 1). Often those called—even in such dramatic ways—initially respond with obstinance or at least resistance before finally accepting their God-given charge.

In Hebrew Scriptures, God's people also are called to a wide variety of specific tasks. God calls Moses and later Deborah to free God's chosen people from their bondage in Egypt and from their oppressors. David and other kings apparently are called to and gifted for the political work of establishing a people and creating order. Gifted women are called to use their skills to create yarns and fine linens for use in Israel's tabernacle worship (Exod. 35:25-26). Other men and women, including Bezalel and Oholiab, are called to use their abilities in the arts and crafts to create the tabernacle (Exod. 31:2-6).

Moses says, "the Lord . . . has filled [these people] with divine spirit, with skill, intelligence, and knowledge in every kind of craft, to devise artistic designs, to work in gold, silver, and bronze, in cutting stones for setting, and in carving wood, and in every kind of craft." As the people's "hearts are stirred," they come to offer their passions in the service of God (Exod. 35:20-35).

In Christian Scriptures we find Mary's calling to bear the Christ in Luke 1 and Jesus' calling of the disciples from their former work into service in his movement.

Among the Greek terms indicating a sense of calling is *ekklesia,* which comes to mean "church" in the New Testament. Ekklesia comes from the Greek *ek,* meaning "from" or "out of," and *klesia,* a form of *klesis* or "calling." Those in the church are those who are "called out ones."[6] Other Greek terms often translated in English as "call" or "calling" include *kalein* (call), *klesis* (calling), and *kletos* (called) and their variations.

In Christian Scriptures calling is used in reference to being called into the kingdom, as in the parable in Matthew 22:1-14 or in Paul's admonition in 1 Thessalonians 2:12 to "lead a life worthy of God, who calls you into [God's] own kingdom and glory." Christians are called to "belong to Jesus Christ" in Romans 1:6, and "to be saints" in the subsequent verse.

In addition to callings into some particular tasks in the body of believers, Christians are called into the fellowship of Christ in 1 Corinthians 1:9; into Christ's freedom in Galatians 5:13 ("For you were called to freedom, brothers and sisters; only do not use your freedom as an opportunity for self-indulgence, but through love become slaves to one another"); and into the peace of Christ, "to which indeed you were called in one body" in Colossians 3:15. Sinners and outsiders are called into God's reign or God's banquet in Matthew 9:12-13 and Luke 14:23.

One of the most fertile passages about calling, in the minds of the sixteenth-century Reformers, comes in Paul's words in 1 Corinthians 7:17-24. The passage comes amid a discussion about circumcision, with Paul urging his hearers to "lead the life that the Lord has assigned, to which God called you. . . . Let each of you remain in the condition in which you were called." As we will see in Chapter Three, these verses form the foundation for Luther's expansive view of calling, a view critiqued by others living in Luther's time and since.

GENERAL AND PARTICULAR CALLINGS

Over the last 500 years or so, a number of Christians have suggested that in Hebrew Scriptures and Christian Scriptures calling or vocation is understood to have two primary meanings. The most pervasive meaning is "the call to become a member of the people of God and to take up the duties that pertain to that membership." Luther understood this as God's "spiritual calling," and the Puritans referred to it as God's "general calling."[7] All Christians are called by God, or called out by God, to become God's people or disciples of Christ.

A second and more contested biblical understanding that most Protestants identify is that of diverse or individual callings, what Luther referred to as God's "external calling" and the Puritans identified as God's "particular calling." In addition to our general calling to be followers of Christ, we are, say some Protestants and Catholics, called by God to specific tasks, roles, offices, or responsibilities within the church and broader society.[8]

Among those critical of such an understanding is author and philosopher Paul Marshall, who argues that the sense of calling "as one's social position, occupation, or anything external, is untenable" in Christian Scriptures. "This means," says Marshall, "that the Bible does not contain a notion of vocation or calling in one of the senses in which these terms were used in Reformation theology."[9]

Similarly, the "vocation" entry in *The Westminster Dictionary of Christian Theology* says that in the New Testament "there is no suggestion that God calls anyone to enter a particular profession or occupation; all those who are called [to the acceptance of salvation and new life in Christ] are expected to show in daily life and work that they are so called."[10] In other words, Christians are called to follow Christ, not to particular jobs or professions. In whatever work they do, Christians should live and work in a way that evidences their commitments.

What seems clear from Christian history is that those who committed themselves to the Jesus movement in its first several centuries recognized the import of that decision of faith, the way in which being a disciple of a crucified Christ would shape the entirety of their lives. As small, often marginalized, and frequently persecuted communities of believers, being committed to Christ and the church generally meant opening themselves to transformation and service as well as making sacrifices, taking risks, and closing doors. The early church understood that such transformation and sacrifice would likely be experienced by all believers, whatever their professions, not just church leaders.

NARROWING OF THE VOCATIONAL SCOPE

From the beginning, of course, there were leaders in the movement—gifted people called out for special tasks—as we can clearly see in Christian Scriptures. As the church spread to new territories and grew in numbers (though still modest in size and still a cultural minority), systems of leadership evolved further, expanding and complicating roles and offices in the church: ministers and bishops and over-bishops. A clear distinction developed between leaders and "laity," the common believers.

The meaning of Christian discipleship and the leader-laity distinction both underwent profound transformation in the years after the Emperor Constantine came into power in 311/312. From the beginning, Constantine openly favored Christianity, believing that the God of this strange sect had delivered the empire to him. Church leaders were granted greater social standing, political power, and cultural influence. New converts flooded into churches, multiplying Christian numbers and simultaneously watering down what it meant to be a follower of Jesus.

Partly in response to this popularizing of Christianity, monasticism became exceedingly popular in the years just after Constantine came into power. Although monasteries and nunneries eventually took on official functions within the church, they began largely as protest movements.[11] Monks and nuns were those who sought a closer relationship with God, a relationship similar to that which nearly all Christians had shared in the earliest centuries of the church: They were those who wanted commitments of faith to still matter, to demand something of them.

And so you have developing by the early fourth century a two-tiered form of commitment to Christ and the church: on the one hand were those who had withdrawn into the monasteries and nunneries coupled with those in official leadership roles in the church, and on the other hand the vast majority of common Christians.[12] Leaders, monks, and nuns became the "religious," those who had a sacred calling or vocation.

As a result, Christian calling became truncated, referring only to those who entered the priesthood or religious orders and devaluing the work of others outside of those confines. The church marched on, gradually reifying this split and spiritually denigrating the day-to-day activities of laypeople. In other words, only people in official church roles were perceived as having Christian vocations—being called by God to some sort of religious work. Regular people's occupations or involvements didn't have any spiritual significance.

Catholicism since the 1960s has given greater theological dignity to broader forms of work, marriage and family, and other earthly affairs, recognizing that they "participate in God's unfolding work of creation and redemption."[13] Even today, though, in both official and popular Catholic literature, the term *calling* usually continues to be applied primarily to church-related activities by designated leaders.[14]

In Chapter 3 we will see how Martin Luther, John Calvin, and the Anabaptists transformed this notion of calling, expanding and altering vocation's scope and meaning.

QUESTIONS FOR REFLECTION

1. What might we learn from Moses' story of calling? Why is it that his initial reluctance to serve God is often overlooked in our telling of salvation history?

2. Why do you think the biblical authors and editors so frequently included stories of reluctant prophets and leaders?

3. For what work or what commitments do you find your heart stirring?

4. How do you respond to church leaders who have suggested that we not only have a general calling to be Christian disciples, but more specific or particular callings to a certain kind of work? Do you consider your past or future occupation or profession to be a particular calling?

5. What is the author suggesting about how the concept of vocation or calling got narrowed in the early Christian centuries?

6. What does it mean to think about monks and nuns as part of "protest movements"? In what ways does your own church represent a "protest movement" in your culture?

Chapter 3

EXPANDING THE SCOPE

Throughout most of the Middle Ages, those recognized as having a sacred calling or vocation—the "religious"—were primarily monks, nuns, and priests. The notion of "vocation" or "calling" became quite narrow, referring only to those in formal churchly roles.

In the sixteenth century, reformer Martin Luther rejected this vocational double standard—as he saw it—as well as his monastic vows, believing that true faith needed to be worked out in the complex and often difficult realities of life beyond monastery walls. He maintained that all "stations" in life in which it is possible to live honestly are divine vocations.

Those honest stations included those which are to be found in the family—to be husband, father, wife, mother, child, friend; those which belonged to the economic order—shopkeeper, milkmaid, laborer; and those which are part of political life—to be queen, governor, or subject. All of these roles, Luther believed, are "masks" of God, faces through which the work of God in human life can be revealed.[15]

The story is told of three stonecutters at work in the same limestone quarry. Every day their work was the same, cutting large blocks of stone. One day a visitor came to the quarry. He asked the first stonecutter, "What are you doing?" The first stonecutter said, "I'm breaking rocks, can't you see?" The visitor then asked the second stonecutter the same question: "What are you doing?" The second worker replied, "I'm doing my job, getting a paycheck to feed my family." Then the visitor asked the third stonecutter: "What are you doing?" The third stonecutter stroked the stone she was cutting, looked up and said, "I'm building a cathedral."[16]

Although all three workers were doing the same task, only the third saw her work in its larger context, recognizing that she was working collaboratively with others to build a beautiful structure. Luther writes,

> What is our work in field and garden, in town and house, in battling and in ruling, to God, but the work of [God's] children. Our works are God's mask, behind which [God] remains hidden, although [God] does all things.[17]

Luther, and later the second-generation reformer John Calvin, drew their understanding of calling in part from the apocryphal book Ecclesiasticus 11:20-21 and from Paul's words in 1 Corinthians 7:20, where the apostle says, "Let each of you remain in the condition in which you were called." Paul precedes this admonition with a discussion of circumcision and follows it by talking about whether as followers of Jesus people were slaves or free when they were called. In verse 24, Paul writes, "In whatever condition you were called, brothers and sisters, remain there with God."

Luther, arguing that there is nothing particularly special about the priestly role, extends for all people the spiritual aura previously ascribed only to clerics, nuns, priests, bishops, and popes.[18] Early twentieth-century sociologist Max Weber argues in *The Protestant Ethic and the Spirit of Capitalism* that this was an "unquestionably new" teaching: "the valuation of the fulfillment of duty in worldly affairs as the highest form which the moral activity of the individual could assume."[19]

Luther writes that "All Christian[20] men are priests and the women priestesses, be they young or old, masters or servants, mistresses or maids, learned or unlearned."[21] Here we have, regarding the church, the germinal concept of the priesthood of all believers—a view that also enters into Anabaptist-Mennonite self-understandings. From Luther's perspective, the everyday worldly activity of everyone in that priesthood of believers has religious significance.

Appointed to Offices, Roles, and Particular Work

According to Luther, God divinely appoints all Christians to their roles and their work, not just those in particular religious positions.[22] One's call to serve God and neighbor came amid her sphere of work; it was not the occupation or profession itself.[23] Vocation required a right use of one's role in the service of others.

Theologian John Calvin, who emerged into religious leadership several decades after Luther, wanted to extend Luther's reforms. He followed in the train of Ulrich Zwingli, who was a contemporary of Luther's and the town priest in Zurich, Switzerland. Presbyterian churches today, as well as other denominations that have "Reformed" in their title, usually are built on Zwingli's and Calvin's teachings. In his own reflections on vocation, Calvin drew from Luther's writings. Often when Calvin uses the term *calling* he is referring simply to a general call to salvation or a specific call to ministry. But Calvin also shares Luther's view that one could live out one's particular Christian calling in more than just traditionally "religious" roles.

Calvin writes that because of the "restlessness" and "fickleness" of human nature, God has appointed duties to every person "lest through our stupidity and rashness everything be turned topsy-turvy." God has named these various kinds of living "callings," says Calvin, "a sort of sentry post so that [we] may not heedlessly wander about throughout life."[24] With only minimal flexibility, Christians are urged to stay in their God-assigned callings.

Similarly, Luther suggests that Christians should take it as a sure sign that they are in the right role or occupation "if you feel disgust and dislike" for the calling. God is simply permitting evil spirits to tempt and attack you, he writes, "to see whether you are fickle or steadfast, or not; and [God] provides an opportunity for your faith to fight and grow stronger."[25] In other words, this was a fairly conservative sense of calling, encouraging people to stay in the roles they had. Hating one's occupation was not necessarily a sign that one should change roles; God might just be testing you to see if you could be steadfast, Luther said.

Both Luther and Calvin saw some occupations and roles as beyond the realm of Christian service. For Calvin, callings needed to be those that were useful to the broader social community; they thus could not include such work as brothel keeper or thief.[26] Utility was essential for something to be considered a calling: Calvin emphasized the "advantage," "utility," "profit," and "fruit" of all Christian work and had a rather expansive view of how this "fruit" may be understood.[27]

God's Work through Human Hands

In Luther's view, such callings could include those that involved the use of coercion, force, or even killing in the exercise of one's duties in one's role. Human beings are not allowed to take the lives of others, but God is free to do so and exercises such freedom through the offices of judge, executioner, and soldier.[28] Judges would fail their vocation if they did not kill and punish, Luther writes in his treatise "The Sermon on the Mount."[29] Humans are to serve God and their neighbors through doing what is required of their role, occupation, or profession, and as such civic leaders, soldiers, and others are not ethically responsible for the harm they may do others if they are working as God's agents.

"By giving heed to the duties imposed by one's vocation," writes Gustaf Wingren, a Luther scholar,

> a person becomes a useful member of the whole body.... [T]he unified and healthy life of the body is sustained through the fact that each member performs its proper function, which is not the same as that of other members.[30]

Such a view restricted Christians' ability to critique what their occupations or professions asked of them; if you were an executioner or a soldier, you simply killed people as expected in your role. That uncritical acceptance of the requirements of some occupations didn't allow for any challenge of the existing social order, or so the Anabaptists perceived.[31]

In Luther's view, then, people are neither saved nor condemned through their work: while they cooperate with God in earthly endeavors, serving as God's "hands" or "coworkers," salvation is entirely a result of God's grace, not their own works. All Christians live in both the kingdom of God and the kingdom of the World, and as such are to use the "spiritual sword" in their churchly involvements and the "temporal sword," when called for, in the exercise of their worldly roles. The "spiritual sword" did not involve any physical violence or coercion, but the "temporal sword" might well require such violence. That, as we will see in the next chapter, made the Anabaptists uneasy about serving in some civic roles.

Although we won't develop it fully here, the Puritans and other more recent Protestant groups built on their Reforming forebears—Luther, Zwingli, and Calvin, most notably—in their expansive views of vocation and calling.

For sixteenth-century mainstream Protestants, nearly any role or occupation or profession could be a place for Christians to be God's agents. No longer was calling understood to be only for the "religious," who entered the priesthood, monasteries, and nunneries. This was an innovation the Anabaptists embraced, but with more reservations than their Lutheran, Zwinglian, and Calvinist counterparts.

QUESTIONS FOR REFLECTION

1. In what ways did Luther help recover some of the biblical meaning of calling or vocation?

2. How does it help you think about your own work if you imagine that God is working through your hands and your gifts?

3. Are you uncomfortable at all with Luther's broad understanding of roles that can be divinely appointed? If so, why is that? If not, how does his perspective alter your view?

4. Are people ethically responsible for their actions—particularly violent ones—if their position or role asks them to punish or kill others?

5. How much should we be guided by the codes or ethics of our occupation or profession? Is that the main thing that determines what is ethical? Why or why not?

6. What tensions do you suppose early Anabaptists had with Luther and Calvin's understandings of vocation?

Chapter 4

COMMITTING TO DISCIPLESHIP

Sixteenth-century Anabaptists generally appreciated the Reformers' honoring of vocations beyond monastic and priestly callings. However, Anabaptist writings tended to be more critical than affirming of Lutheran and Calvinist understandings, hedging back from the nearly all-inclusive blessing of Christians' involvements.

The Anabaptists were suspicious, for instance, of Luther's perspective on vocation, which they understood to be that a Christian should bring to her vocational role her loving intention, integrity, industriousness, and modesty, but that the content of her activity in that role or profession—what she actually does—"does not come from [her] faith in Jesus but from the 'orders of creation.'"[32] In other words, the Anabaptists thought that observing how the world was presently ordered was not sufficient: Jesus sometimes calls his followers to a different way of being in the world, an upside-down kingdom.

Most Anabaptists were particularly fearful of occupational roles that involved coercive force or violence. Since military service and most political offices required some level of coercion or violence, those were particularly troubling professions or roles. Many Anabaptists, especially the Hutterites, also were deeply suspicious of any work having to do with trade or commerce since those roles in the developing economy might—and often did—involve exploiting workers or consumers of goods.

In the turmoil of the sixteenth century, religious and political officials were concerned with people and groups that threatened whatever minimal order existed.[33] The Anabaptists were speaking radically about both the government and the economic system. They were outspoken about economic injustice, especially when priests and monks were responsible for such injustice.

The Anabaptists also generally agreed that in God's kingdom there should be no "mine" and "thine," and the Hutterite branch developed this into a complete community of goods. Anabaptists were concerned about the equal distribution of goods and worried about the exploitation of the poor by the rich. Having an entire community share their wages and expenses, as was true for the Hutterites, was one extreme way of eliminating economic injustice within that particular body of believers.

While the Anabaptists did not expect their convictions to be adopted by the whole society, their manner of living and their public pronouncements about oppression of the poor represented a threat to the stability of society.[34] The Anabaptist leaders, political officials believed, might undermine both the political and economic order through their "seditious" ramblings about the poor and through their refusal to cooperate with those wielding governmental power. By not baptizing their infants into the state church, for instance, they challenged political officials' ability to keep track of newborn citizens and levy corresponding taxes.

POLITICAL DISENGAGEMENT

Although some Mennonites and others have depicted the Anabaptists' withdrawal from political involvement as a unique attempt at social change, it is more likely that—at least once they established their radical religious boundaries—they were politically disengaged because noninvolvement was their only option. They didn't set out to be withdrawn from society, in other words, but by making some other choices about following Christ, they were unable to participate in some societal roles.

Canadian sociologist Leo Driedger argues that the Anabaptists

> refused to participate in [holding political or civic offices] usually because they did not have a choice, so they withdrew to what they considered more pressing matters. . . . Because of their radical religious and discipleship views, the early Anabaptists had their hands more full trying to find a means of survival.[35]

They needed to keep a low cultural profile, and that meant withdrawal, which limited their options for civic and professional involvements.[36]

From the earliest days of Anabaptism, there was tension with civil authorities over a range of issues. In Zurich, budding Anabaptists were frustrated with town priest Ulrich Zwingli's apparent compromise with the Zurich Town Council in requiring all babies in the canton to be baptized. This was a fusion of churchly matters (whether one was baptized or not) with political powers that the Anabaptists could not tolerate. By the time of the writing of the Schleitheim Confession in 1527—the earliest Anabaptist confession of faith—Anabaptists unabashedly describe "the sword," or political leadership that involves coercive force, as "outside the perfection of Christ." While "outside the perfection of Christ" did not mean "demonic," it did mean, according to the confession, that Christians ought not be civil authorities (magistrates).

The Schleitheim writers, led by former Benedictine monk Michael Sattler, write that

> it does not befit a Christian to be a magistrate: the rule of the government is according to the flesh, that

of the Christians according to the spirit. Their houses and dwelling remain in this world, that of the Christians is in heaven. Their citizenship is in this world, that of the Christians is in heaven.[37]

For the most part, the Anabaptists believed with their Protestant peers that the state was divinely instituted. However, because the civil realm often required the use of violence for maintaining order, most Anabaptists saw political office as beyond the pale for "true Christians." Some Anabaptist leaders—among them Menno Simons (after whom Mennonites are named) and Hans Denck—indicate some ambivalence on this point, although they also believed that the tension in being both a Christian and a magistrate would make life difficult for the true believer. Even Anabaptist leader Pilgram Marpeck, who himself served as a civil engineer, said, in effect, that one could be a Christian magistrate, but not for long—over time, one would need to give up either being a Christian or a magistrate.[38]

DEMANDS IN WORLDLY ROLES

Marpeck's perspective was not that simply being a political authority ran against the grain of discipleship, but that too many of the magistrate's "worldly acts" are contrary to God's will and Christ's Spirit. Christian wisdom does not suit Christians for the magistrate's office, says Marpeck, since it "brings about only grace, mercy, love for the enemy, spiritual supernatural things, cross, tribulation, patience, and faith in Christ without coercion. . . . " Worldly rulers' wisdom governs through the "external sword in vindictiveness, mercilessness, hatred of the enemy, physical vengeance, [and] killing of evildoers."[39]

Marpeck and Denck both believed that insofar as a Christian could govern by the law of Christian love, "limited, benign government service" could be allowed for Christians. Marpeck, though, apparently recognized this as essentially impossible, and accepted exile repeatedly when his own principles were violated in his role as a civil servant.[40]

Hutterite leader Peter Riedemann, while seeing the office of government as "appointed and instituted by God," and therefore "right and good," also views it as having been established because people turned away from God and lived according to their own desires. This view fits a general sixteenth-century Protestant understanding that God put civil authorities in place after humanity's fall, believing that human sin needed to be kept at bay by sword-wielding governing officials. Echoing what many others said, Riedemann writes, "Governmental authority was given in wrath, so it cannot find a place in Christ or be part of him. No Christian is a ruler and no ruler is a Christian, for the child of blessing cannot be the servant of wrath."[41]

An exception to this general Anabaptist understanding of political authorities was Balthasar Hubmaier, reputed to be the "most learned and most gifted communicator"[42] among the early Anabaptists. Hubmaier, the only early Anabaptist leader to have a doctorate in theological studies, was not a pacifist, and as such essentially was written outside the Anabaptist fold by twentieth-century Mennonite historian Harold S. Bender and some of his contemporaries.[43] Hubmaier was baptized two months after the formal beginnings of Anabaptism and martyred at the stake in Vienna less than three years later (1528).

Hubmaier writes that "just as Christ wanted to do justice to his office on earth, likewise we should fulfill our office and calling, be it in government or in obedience, for we shall have to give account of it to God on the last day."[44] Sounding more like Zwingli and Luther than his Anabaptist siblings, Hubmaier says Christians may "with good conscience sit in court and council and may judge and decide also in temporal matters," "punish the unjust," and even "carry the sword in God's place over the evildoer and punish him."[45] This text, taken from "On the Sword," was written in 1527, probably several months after the writing of the Schleitheim Confession.[46] Although Hubmaier's position was among those circulating in Anabaptist communities, his particular view of "offices" and "calling" in relation to political and civic leadership did not survive in Anabaptism after his early martyrdom.

In contemporary Mennonite communities in the United States, Canada, Paraguay, and elsewhere, twenty-first century Mennonites often serve as members of city councils or as county commissioners, differentiating these political roles from the more "sword-wielding" roles at state, provincial, or national levels. In towns such as Goshen, Indiana, it is not unusual for the city council to be populated with half or more people with Anabaptist roots.

TENSIONS WITH BUSINESS AND ECONOMICS

As has been suggested throughout these chapters, Anabaptist understandings of discipleship or the "holy life" meant that social, economic, and ethical matters were integrally related to "spiritual life." Economic activities of believers were to be carried out according to the norms of God's kingdom, which included "sufficiency (not surplus) and the sharing of surplus with those in need."[47] That meant no person or family should have more than they needed for food, shelter, and other essentials, and if they did, they should share their surplus with neighbors.

Early Anabaptists clung to the medieval church's convictions against charging interest for loans to other Christians, a practice forbidden by Roman Church law during the Middle Ages. Among Reformers, they were not alone in this concern.[48] Over time, though, most Protestants progressively allowed for the charging of interest to other Christians as they moved toward the secular economic world of capitalism, which is based on the accumulation of capital.[49]

More generally, most of the Anabaptists discouraged the engagement of true believers in any forms of trade or commerce other than marketing their own crafts. In "True Christian Faith," Menno Simons cites favorably the apocryphal passage Ecclesiasticus[50] 26:29-27:3: "A merchant can hardly keep from wrongdoing, nor is a tradesman innocent of sin. . . . As a stake is driven firmly into a fissure between stones, so sin is wedged in between selling and buying."

Some merchants, says Simons, become thieves, murderers, and holdup men, gamblers, betrayers, brothel keepers, executioners and tormenters, all for the sake of profit. "The whole world is so affected and involved in this accursed avarice, fraud, false practice, and unlawful means of support; in this false traffic and merchandise, with this finance, usury and personal advancement that I do not know how it could get much worse," says Simons. "Yet they continue to be the priests' and preachers' Christians, and then call this earning their bread honestly, and doing justice to all."[51]

To be fair, we have to recognize that Simons takes a swipe at lots of other folks in this passage, too—among them lords and princes, judges, lawyers, and advocates, and priests, monks, and preachers. In his references to "wicked merchants and retailers," Simons adds parenthetically, "I say the wicked, for I do not mean those who are righteous and pious."[52]

Hutterite Peter Riedemann's words are equally harsh regarding certain kinds of merchants. He says his Hutterite communities do not allow any of their members to be traders or merchants, since "this is a sinful business." Riedemann has no problem with buying what is necessary for the needs of one's house or craft and then using the materials to create something new that is then sold. "This is no sin," he says.[53] In fact, "God will be praised and our industry and conscientiousness recognized in work that is honestly done," in creating things that are needed by our neighbors. Hutterites were not to participate in producing frivolous items—those that served pride, ostentation, or vanity.[54] But they could certainly practice their crafts in producing goods essential for living.

From Riedemann's perspective, what is clearly wrong, though, "is to buy an article and sell it for a profit in the same condition as one bought it. This makes the article more expensive for the poor; it is stealing bread from their mouths and forcing them to become nothing but slaves to the rich."[55] (Perhaps in our contemporary context it would be a little like picking up an item at a garage sale on the cheap, and selling it on eBay for a quick profit, without adding value—a practice which is generally admired.) Riedemann also says members of the church cannot be public innkeepers who serve beer or wine "since this is associated with much that is depraved and godless."

Swiss Anabaptists in Strasbourg in 1568 also recognized the danger of being in some forms of business. They agreed that "No brother shall engage in buying or building or other large (unnecessary) business dealing without the counsel, knowledge, and consent of the brethren and bishops."[56] Canadian Mennonite historian C. Arnold Snyder says, without nuance, "[T]here were to be no Swiss Brethren, Hutterite, or Mennonite financiers or entrepreneurs!"[57]

Sixteenth-century Anabaptists had many concerns about political service and economics that no longer resonate fully with their twenty-first-century ancestors. However, we need to understand their concerns for certain occupational and professional roles and consider the ways in which any of our involvements exploit others, or do violence to others. Such concerns remain relevant five centuries after they were first articulated by the Anabaptists—and twenty centuries after they were embodied in Jesus.

QUESTIONS FOR REFLECTION

1. As mentioned in this chapter, many Mennonites in the U.S., Canada, Paraguay, and elsewhere have served on local city councils. In Canada, Mennonites often serve in provincial governments, and in Paraguay a regular participant (though not a member) at a Mennonite church has occupied the nation's highest office. Is political service at these levels appropriate for those in the Anabaptist tradi-

tion? Why or why not? Should contemporary Christians differentiate between local and national political service?

2. How has the world changed in ways that elicit different political responses from contemporary Mennonites than from their Anabaptist forebears? How have Mennonites changed?

3. Are the changes you noted in question 2 good changes? Or just realistic and practical ones? What has been gained, and what has been lost, in shifting Mennonite understandings of political or civic service? If you are from another denominational group, what do you know about changing perceptions of vocation in that denomination?

4. Early Anabaptists had harsh words to say about many business practices (charging interest, reelling a product without adding value, etc.) that we now consider fairly acceptable, even routine. What does this suggest about how Mennonites have changed? Have Mennonites unduly compromised their economic value of sufficiency, or simply come to a more realistic understanding of business?

5. Based on your learnings in the last two chapters, would you say sixteenth-century Anabaptists were right in challenging Luther's and Calvin's blessings of almost any role, office, or profession? Why or why not?

6.What language might Christians use today to describe work that is "outside the perfection of Christ"? What does that language mean to you, if anything?

Chapter 5

CHANGING PASSIONS AND PRACTICES

Skeptical views about merchants and traders expressed by Mennonite leader Menno Simons, Hutterite theologian Peter Riedemann, and the Strasbourg Anabaptists of the sixteenth century contrast greatly with views of some more recent Anabaptist writers and thinkers. Several years ago Mennonite Economic Development Associates hosted a conference titled "Business as a Calling."[58] The following year, Mennonite journalist Wally Kroeker wrote a piece titled "The Wealthy in the Land," which addresses the relative wealth of contemporary U.S. Mennonites, drawing on sociological data and anecdotal information.

Kroeker writes that the feeling that money is wicked "has softened in Mennonite circles." Increasingly, says, Kroeker, "money is seen as a tool for potential good. Another shift has been a growing sense that 'wealth redistribution' is not the only way to handle excess but that 'wealth creation' is a useful way to produce economic opportunity."[59]

The former is a reference to giving away your excess money (which is what sixteenth-century Anabaptists seemingly implied). The latter suggests using surplus money to develop new business ventures or expand existing ones to generate new jobs.

Kroeker notes that this shift among contemporary Mennonites was symbolized in the publication of Mennonite and Brethren in Christ scholar Ron Sider's twentieth-anniversary edition of *Rich Christians in an Age of Hunger*, a "Bible of wealth distribution." In the twentieth-anniversary edition, says Kroeker, Sider provides a "ringing endorsement" of wealth creation through programs such as microenterprise assistance as a way of making a dent in poverty.[60]

Valuing "wealth creation" still makes some contemporary Mennonites squirm; at a minimum, it indicates a dramatic shift away from the radical economic views of sixteenth-century Anabaptists.[61]

Canadian sociologists and economists Calvin Redekop, Victor A. Krahn, and Samuel J. Steiner thoughtfully address these economic developments in their book *Anabaptist-Mennonite Faith and Economics*, perhaps the best treatment of historical and contemporary perspectives on Mennonites and business.[62] Mennonite historian Arnold Snyder's essay in that text asks, "Were the Anabaptists wrong, mistaken, or misguided in their understanding of the spiritual life, and the way in which they saw the spiritual life relating to economic life?"

Snyder continues,

> Do we have a clearer understanding today than they did in the sixteenth century of what the true spiritual life requires with regard to economic life? Or have we unwittingly made concessions in our spiritual life to accommodate economic practices we do not know how to live without?[63]

Another piece in the same volume by philosopher and former Goshen College president J. Lawrence Burkholder provides his own responses to such questions, arguing that the reason followers of Christ may enter the marketplace of money, power, competition, and litigation is that "it is through enterprise that people find work, build homes, and eat." We live in an ambiguous world, argues Burkholder, caught between the ideal and the real.[64]

ANABAPTIST OCCUPATIONS

In terms of their actual work, the earliest Anabaptists primarily were drawn from the craft and farming occupations. The missioners who spread the movement were largely craftspeople, who could be quite mobile.[65] One study of Anabaptist occupational roles estimated that 41 percent were craftspeople in cities, small towns, and villages, and just under 24 percent were farmers.[66] Within two generations, the percentages shifted dramatically as Anabaptists, under persecution, were driven to rural areas and into primarily land-based occupations. In other words, while Anabaptists emerged in a rich academic and theological milieu, the Anabaptist movement quickly moved through the merchant classes and then to the peasantry. With increasing persecution of Anabaptists in sixteenth-century Europe, within short order Anabaptism became a purely rural phenomenon, with few Anabaptist craftspeople remaining in the cities.[67]

Up until the middle of the sixteenth century, almost twice as many Anabaptists were in larger cities as in small country towns, but during the second half of the century most larger cities ostracized Anabaptists.[68] Anabaptists in towns and villages also refused to participate in craft guilds (organizations of people doing particular crafts), which in turn became hostile to Anabaptists. Within a very short period, then, Anabaptists made their homes and their livings almost entirely in rural communities.

Throughout the following several centuries, after the initiation of the Anabaptist movement in Europe's urban centers, most Mennonites outside of the Dutch and North German context[69] spent their time and energies in rural communities and in agriculture-related occupations. Dutch and North German Mennonites more quickly integrated into their cultural contexts, working in business and the arts and other professions.

However, Swiss and South German Anabaptists, less willing to accommodate to their cultures than their northern counterparts, and persecuted by civil authorities for a longer period, did not settle into urban cultural contexts with such ease. "For 300 years farming was thought to be *the* Mennonite way of life and the rural community the indispensable form of organizing their common life," says Mennonite historian C. J. Dyck.[70] Many Mennonites believed it would be impossible to survive as Mennonites in the cities, or that they would need to unduly compromise their Christian principles in such settings.

Not all Mennonites were engaged in this "sacred vocation"[71] of farming, though, contrary to what some have believed. Unlike later Mennonites, most of the original Germantown, Pennsylvania, Mennonite settlers in 1683 were craftspeople and tradespeople, with the majority apparently being linen weavers.[72] Mennonite settlements in early eighteenth-century American colonies often included—in addition to farmers—bricklayers, millers, weavers, and other tradespeople, and even the rare physician.[73] Often farmers practiced a craft in addition to farming their land, and by the middle of the eighteenth century Mennonites were prominent in the crafts in the American colonies.[74]

Colonial Mennonites avoided ocean shipping and military service. The church also, according to a 1773 letter of Mennonites to Europe, discouraged officeholding, "because force is used therein," and innkeeping, "because it leads to a great number of irregularities." Aside from those few exclusions, "the occupational pattern of Mennonites in colonial Pennsylvania scarcely differed from the patterns of Scotch-Irish Presbyterians or of German Lutherans."[75]

MAJOR SHIFTS IN OCCUPATIONAL PATTERNS

In North America, the more extensive Mennonite shift from small-town crafts and farming to the professions and the office took place rapidly—between the early 1950s and the late 1970s, with the shift from the field to professions often bypassing factory and other blue-collar work.[76]

Along the way, certainly, Mennonites continued to practice the trades, as they have since the sixteenth century. They have been contractors, plumbers, butchers, millers, electricians, and furniture-makers, and they have been appreciated for their artistry, efficiency, and dependability. In each of these roles, they have functioned as essentially self-employed owners, or at least people who participated in management decisions as quasi-owners, just as they have done since their early days of farming for European lords.

For ethnic North American Mennonites, what has been largely missed in our history of work is the experience of labor—punching a time clock, and having little or no control over the products of our labor. That skews our lived reality in relation to vocation. We ought not forget, as Mennonite business consultant David Schrock-Shenk says, that

> we have held relatively privileged positions in the world of capitalism, obscured by our ethnic myths of persecution, diaspora, and dispossession. We have been self-employed, owners of the means of production, held capital, and worked in professions . . . that are relatively autonomous and held in high social esteem.[77]

Now, with the broadening of the Mennonite family in North America, with the expanding racial, ethnic, and socio-economic diversity in Anabaptist-Mennonite churches, and with greater awareness of the majority Mennonite cultures south of the equator, Mennonites are ever-so-slowly getting a window into the underside of vocational history.[78]

TRAINING TEACHERS AND HEALTH CARE WORKERS

Since the late nineteenth century, Mennonite colleges had been training a host of professionals, educating thousands of teachers by the 1950s[79] and a host of others in health-related fields.[80] But the numbers of Mennonite young people entering professions, and the fields that they entered, expanded dramatically during the latter half of the twentieth century.

Part of the reason for this expansion was the exposure Mennonites had to other occupational fields and professions through alternative service work—doing some kind of domestic or international social service instead of serving in the military. Among those alternative programs were Civilian Public Service (CPS) in the 1940s, I-W service in the 1950s, and Voluntary Service, which began under Mennonite Central Committee auspices in the 1940s and expanded into denomination-specific programs thereafter.

"In the vanguard of the new change was a younger generation schooled in CPS and postwar voluntary service and building on the mid-twentieth-century intellectual reconstruction of Mennonite history," writes Mennonite historian Paul Toews. "That generation was moving the church toward a more clearly defined theology of service and a more globally engaged missional identity."[81]

Mennonites also have entered professions in the arts previously discounted by their communities—as poets, novelists, visual artists, actors, journalists, and filmmakers. In her essay on "Bringing Home the Work" in *The Body and the Book*, poet Julia Kasdorf talks about tensions with becoming one of the "liars and rascals" in her field[82]—people who write fiction (lies) and sometimes push the church's boundaries by writing honestly about human fallibility. Many Mennonites entered the arts slowly, painfully, receiving little encouragement from their homes or the church.

The shift toward professionalism, often associated with the move toward suburbia and urban centers, was a serious point of tension between the 1940s and 1960s in U.S.-American Mennonite life. *Mennonite Quarterly Review* ran a series of articles in its July 1942 issue growing out of a Mennonite Sociology Conference the previous December.

Sociologist Ernst Correll writes there that Mennonite traditions in faith and practice "grew and bore fruit mainly in an environment of rural life and town handicraft economy." Among "genuine Mennonite groups," says Correll, agricultural occupations predominate, just as they always have.

> Records of more emphatically *urban* Mennonite communities as well as of any fringe of Mennonite life that fell under the spell of progressive urbanization, however, bear shocking witness to gradual decline, if not complete extinction.[83]

By the first decade of the twenty-first century, only 12 percent of U.S. Mennonite adults lived on a farm, compared with three times that many in the early 1970s. During that same period the number of Mennonites in professional and technical roles increased rapidly, expanding as these occupational roles emerged and went through their own transformations. Today 41 percent of U.S. Mennonites are in managerial and professional occupations, and 27 percent are in technical, sales, and administrative support roles.

The entry of massive numbers of Mennonite women into the workforce marked yet another dramatic transformation in the North American occupational landscape in the last fifty years. Today only eight percent of U.S. Mennonites identify themselves as housewives/homemakers.[84] The changing roles of women altered the nature of parenting, strengthened household incomes in homes with two working parents and changed some of the power dynamics in the household.

Whatever North American Mennonites may have believed about vocation, they dramatically expanded their actual work in the world over the last half-century. Most of that expansion included moves into business, professional occupations, and a broader array of fields. In this chapter we have simply been noting those sociological shifts, but in subsequent chapters we will address some of the ethical questions related to these changing work experiences.

QUESTIONS FOR REFLECTION

1. What do you think of the shifting emphasis from "wealth redistribution" to "wealth creation"? Is this a positive change? A realistic one?

2. Do you agree with J. Lawrence Burkholder that we live in an ambiguous world, caught between the ideal and the real?

3. If the world is somewhat ambiguous, what has that meant in your own life's work, or in the work you would like to do someday? Can you think of any examples where you have been caught between the ideal and the real?

4. How do you think the move from farms to factories, schools, and health care facilities has affected Mennonite culture? What do you know about these shifts in other denominational groups, or in North America more generally?

5. Where do you see important compromises in what you read above? What compromises make you a little uncomfortable? Why is that?

6. Have artists had a particularly difficult time finding their place in Mennonite churches? If so, why is that? How do other Christian groups view their artists and writers?

Chapter 6

BLESSING THE OCCUPATIONAL SHIFT

Former Mennonite Board of Missions administrator John W. Eby once said his first conscious experience with professionalism was asking his parents why it was that when people from his Lititz, Pennsylvania, congregation became successful businessmen, teachers, or doctors, they left the Mennonite church to become Lutherans, Brethren, or Evangelical United Brethren.[85] In some past decades, Mennonites who were financially or professionally successful felt awkward in their Mennonite congregations, which didn't automatically approve of their "success."

Nonetheless, as Mennonites—both men and women— increasingly moved into the professions in the 1950s, 1960s, and 1970s, churchly endorsements of this shift appeared in print and at conferences. Clearly our theology responds to social and economic shifts, as it should. The last thing Mennonites need is a theology dissociated from the lived experiences of Mennonite people. But if the last thing we need is a disconnected and unrelated theology of vocation, the next-to-last thing we need is a theology that simply and uncritically blesses the socio-economic trajectories of the majority of North American Mennonites. The danger is allowing theology to be held unduly captive to the interests of middle- and middle-upper-class Mennonites.

In the 1940s and early 1950s, Mennonite sociologist Guy F. Hershberger and others sought to strengthen rural Mennonite communities through the Mennonite Community Association (organized in 1946) and a short-lived journal called *The Mennonite Community*, calling Mennonites to return to their rural roots.[86]

By 1956, however, in a speech at the Mennonite Student Fellowship in Philadelphia, Pennsylvania, the plain-coated E. E. Miller, former president of Goshen College, endorses young Mennonites' entrée into various professions. He defines a profession as a "vocation [that] requires extended and arduous training" and "requires of its practitioners personal commitment to an existing ethical code." Miller says "excellence of performance and extent of service offered to the community" set before the profession an excellent ideal. Miller notes, in his 1950s context, that by far the largest professional group in the church is teachers, but he also references the growing numbers of doctors, nurses and social workers. He argues that there is a "great opportunity within the professions for the exercise of a true Christian ethic" that counters the dishonesty, profit-seeking, and power-grabbing that conditions so much of what makes up Christians' working lives.

In this spirit, Miller encourages his student listeners to view their profession as a "Christian calling." He draws on Jesus' parable of the talents to speak of Mennonites' stewardship of their gifts. "So have no fears," says Miller to his audience of graduate students. "Go ahead and prepare. The church needs you and today's world offers you many opportunities to serve in the name of Christ."[87]

ANALYZING THE MOVE TOWARD PROFESSIONALISM

Two additional conferences took place in the 1970s, the first sponsored by Eastern Area Mennonite Student Services and titled "Professionalism: Faith, Ethics, and Christian Identity." Mennonite theologian Gordon Kaufman gave a plenary address at that conference in which he critiqued the sectarian consciousness of Mennonites who see the world outside the church as "sinful, fallen, and dangerous."

Such a closed-group-consciousness worked, Kaufman says, as long as Mennonites lived in somewhat closed communities. "But in modern professional life it makes no sense at all. Our lives are lived for the most part outside the confines of the church." Moreover, Kaufman argues that

> if we are going to be professionals today our lives will be lived "in the world" in a much fuller sense than many earlier Mennonites would have regarded as legitimate, and the norms and standards in which we make decisions in our professions will be drawn from our experience in the world.[88]

Kaufman moves toward a cautious and critical embrace of traditional Mennonite notions of love and self-sacrifice, reconciliation and community, and devotion and service to God. The details of what those principles will look like in our professions will vary, and we must be willing to question them in light of other knowledge, says Kaufman. "We must be prepared to open up our Mennonitism to attitudes and practices unknown in the past, to help enable it to become a vital and significant force in the new situation in the present in which we are living and into which we are moving."[89]

Mennonite Student and Young Adult Services hosted another conference the following year, in February 1979, titled "Conflict in the World of Professions." Sociologist Paul Peachey gave a plenary address on "Profession, Person, and Common Good" that was perhaps more nuanced than Kaufman's from the previous year and more attentive to the conflicts inherent within professionalism—maintaining monopolies, promoting and defending the economic self-interest of their members, using "professional ethics" as a fig leaf to hide their economic greed.[90]

Three years after the 1979 conference sociologist Don Kraybill and publisher Phyllis Pellman Good, both professionals themselves, edited a thoughtful text titled *Perils of Professionalism: Essays on Christian Faith and Professionalism*. In their introduction to the collection of stories by professionals in a variety of fields, Kraybill and Pellman Good write that the chief peril is that "professions have an uncanny tendency to subvert their original good intentions": professions tend toward serving their own vested interests, dominating and controlling their members, serving the profession more than their clients, and even professionalizing the church and dominating its decision-making process.[91] The same year Pellman Good wrote in an op-ed piece in *The Philadelphia Inquirer*, "I believe that true community and professions are adversaries."[92]

PROFESSIONALISM AND MENNONITE IDENTITY: WHO ARE WE NOW?

In the years since the two young adult conferences in Philadelphia and New York City, and the publication of *The Perils of Professionalism*, little has been written or attended to in the Mennonite world regarding the general topic of professionalism. In the decade following the mini-explosion of professionalism conferences and writings, North American Mennonites seemingly turned their attention away from the topic of professionalism, save for a noteworthy and under-used book titled *Who Am I? What Am I? Searching for Meaning in Your Work*,[93] by sociologist Calvin Redekop and consultant Urie A. Bender. For the past thirty years, Redekop has been at the forefront of many of the key Mennonite projects addressing professionalism, work, and business.

For the most part, though, by the late 1980s Mennonites turned their attention away from the general topic of professionalism and toward the related topic of Mennonite identity. Between 1987 and 1990, at least six books were published with titles such as *Anabaptist-Mennonite Identi-*

ties in Ferment, Mennonite Identity in Conflict, and *Mennonite Identity.*[94] Those texts were forerunners to Leo Driedger and J. Howard Kauffman's *Mennonite Mosaic,*[95] which further pluralized Mennonite identity through a detailed sociological survey.

Within specific professions, a range of texts has been published in recent years, perhaps primarily regarding ministry[96] and business[97] but also in the fields of medical ethics. Mennonites also have turned their attention to the related question of power in journal articles and texts such as Benjamin Redekop and Calvin Redekop's *Power, Authority, and the Anabaptist Tradition.*[98]

REMEMBERING THE TENSIONS

Mennonites need to continue to reflect on the tensions, conflicts, and possibilities within their work. They also need to recognize how women, and often those in racially underrepresented groups in North America, have had more limited occupational options. Middle-aged and older Mennonite women can testify to a long history of having few options for Christian service presented to them in their growing-up years. In church roles, such restrictions are still true in the many Mennonite congregations who do not accept women as pastors.

On the other side of these limitations, some Mennonites who came to Canada from Russia in the early twentieth century told an interviewer they had come to Canada with "nothing" and had then become successful businesspeople and professionals. But in reality they had come with more than nothing: They had arrived with a memory of financial success and wealth, a knowledge of how to run a business, and a belief in themselves and their ability to pull themselves up.[99]

That Russian Mennonite experience contrasts greatly with that of African-American Mennonites (and other African-Americans) who were enslaved for generations, not allowed to make decisions, not provided with educational opportunities, and told they were worthless. Generations of such treatment make for dramatically different occupational and professional opportunities.[100]

As Mennonites speak about callings and vocation, they need to be aware of these power and experiential dynamics and bring these real-world experiences into their theological considerations. Mennonites also need to be aware of their history in relation to restricting and then blessing certain occupations. As Mennonites moved into the professions, they hosted a series of conferences addressing ethical issues related to such a shift, but since the 1970s only minimal attention has been paid to "the perils of professionalism."

QUESTIONS FOR REFLECTION

1. Why do you suppose church leaders began to support many young people who were moving into professional roles?

2. In *The Perils of Professionalism,* Don Kraybill and Phyllis Pellman Good write that "professions have an uncanny tendency to subvert their original good intentions." What did they mean by that?

3. Do you agree or disagree with Kraybill and Pellman Good in the quote above? Have you had experiences in which your profession or occupation seemed to move away from its original good intentions?

4. What impact has professionalism had on Anabaptist-Mennonite identity?

5. How is the public perception of what it means to be Mennonite different than the Mennonite reality, and what part does vocation have in that?

6. Have you ever felt restricted, by your gender, race, ethnicity, family expectations, or other factors, from serving in certain occupations? Why is that? How might you, or how did you, expand possibilities for yourself and others of your generation?

Chapter 7

LINGERING AMBIGUITY
REGARDING MINISTRY

As one who teaches at a church institution and is committed to the church, I am exceedingly conscious of my responsibility to call out gifted young people for service not only in the world but also in the church. That's a responsibility all of us have—to encourage young people to offer their gifts to the church as active members and leaders. That means calling people to be pastors, or missionaries, or employees in our church institutions. When those of us who are older see young people with gifts of leadership, or gifts that could be used full-time in service to God, God calls us to do the essential shoulder-tapping, nurturing, and developing of those gifts.

This has sometimes been tough for the church and difficult for twenty-first-century parents as well, as I have already discovered. During the early months that I was working on this book, our family was living in Puerto Rico. One day our oldest son Niles and I were driving into the capital city, and we began talking about his life and about what he wanted to do with his energies and passions.

Niles' childhood experience is odd in that by the end of sixth grade he had been in seven different schools in five different countries because of our traveling for my teaching work. My spouse and I had led semester-long college study groups in China, Dominican Republic, Cuba, Costa Rica, and Cambodia, and also lived one autumn in Puerto Rico. For Niles, having a life work where he can travel internationally is essential.

That fall day, as Niles and I were driving to a doctor's appointment in San Juan, Niles asked me what sorts of things he could do that would allow him to travel—other than being a professor, which he thought looked extremely boring when his kindergarten class visited my college classroom some years earlier.

I mentioned that he could be a travel writer for a newspaper or magazine, and that that would also use his writing skills. Or he could be in certain types of businesses that allow for or require travel. As I was thinking of various other options, Niles said, "What about being a missionary?" And I was struck by how—amid a research project on vocation and amid a life where I have encouraged scores of students to consider churchly vocations—I had neglected to mention at the top of my list international work in the service of Christ and the church.

We then talked at length about how that would be a wonderful option, allowing him to learn to know a particular culture and people very well, possibly allowing him to use his technological interests and skills or his desires to be a pilot. We also talked about how, when choosing a particular profession or vocation, one needs to consider whether deep desire (in Niles' case, his passion for international travel and cross-cultural experiences) is worked into the occupation itself, or whether one does another sort of work that provides enough income and flexibility to allow for travel beyond one's specific job.

An integrated life, I suggested, was much better: one in which one's day-to-day work is an expression of one's deep desire. We then talked about needing to listen for God's call, and how that call was often discovered as we followed our passions—and discerned the world's needs.

ANABAPTISTS AND MINISTRY

As mentioned in earlier chapters, sixteenth-century Anabaptists felt some ambivalence not only about the more general concept of vocation but also its specific application to ministry. That ambivalence has continued through most of Anabaptist-Mennonite history and is likely a reality Mennonites will continue to live with through at least the early decades of the twenty-first century.

Initial Anabaptist ambivalence about churchly vocations is rooted partly in the biblical texts, though as we will see below the Anabaptists frequently cite Christian Scriptures to talk about churchly roles. Greater contributing factors to this dis-ease with churchly vocations are the social and political dynamics of the sixteenth century.

Relatively early on, the Anabaptists developed an anti-clerical posture, prompted largely by their tense relationships with both Protestant and Catholic clergy, who were among the learned who condemned many early Anabaptists to martyrdom.[101] Such a posture was directed primarily at those outside their Anabaptist communities; in contrast, most Anabaptist ministers were believed to have experienced a true, spiritual call.[102]

Further complicating Anabaptist understandings of ministry were aberrations within the fellowship itself from those who claimed to have received a direct prophetic call. And, adding to a guarded endorsement of ministry was a partial embrace of the "priesthood of all believers"[103] espoused by other Reformers.[104]

LEADING THE EARLY ANABAPTISTS

In the Anabaptist movement's early years, a good number of leaders were drawn from the clergy and were relatively well educated; however, most of these leaders were killed within the first several years of the movement.[105] That resulted in a relatively plural leadership in the church—having many people serve in leadership. That was perhaps a development prompted by making a virtue out of a necessity. Since there were few strong, literate leaders, everyone needed to help out in the church.

After twenty-one Anabaptists were arrested in 1562 while worshipping in a ravine, court records indicate they were repeatedly asked who their leader was. "Well," they say, "our last leader died three years ago, in 1559." And then they go on to explain that Brother John sometimes reads Scripture, and Hans sometimes provides interpretation, but so do Christian and George, and sometimes Felix reads Scripture, too.[106] They may simply have been protecting their leaders, but it's safe to assume that the sixteenth-century Anabaptists did have plural leadership. At some points these were people "called out" for specific tasks, and at other times leadership was likely more informal.

Hutterite Peter Riedmann, in his *Confession of Faith*, identifies assorted offices in the church, drawing at each point on Scripture: apostles (Rom. 1:1-5 and 16:25-27); bishops and shepherds (1 Tim. 3:1-7 and Titus 1:5-9); helpers (1 Cor. 12:4-8); rulers, who "direct each person, whether in the home or in church, so that everything is done correctly and well" (Rom. 12:4-8 and 1 Corinthians 12:1-11 and 14:40); and finally, elders, "who serve in the church wherever and however need requires" (Acts 15:2-6).[107]

The Schleitheim Confession, already referred to in previous chapters, designates a role for "shepherds in the church of God." Such a shepherd, say the writers of the 1527 document, should be a person "who has a good report of those who are outside the faith," and whose role shall be

> to read and exhort and teach, warn, admonish, or ban in the congregation, and properly to preside among the sisters and brothers in prayer, and in the breaking of bread, and in all things to take care of the body of Christ. . . .

Shepherds should be supported by the congregation as they have need, and if they should be driven away or martyred, "at the same hour another shall be ordained to his place, so that the little folk and the little flock of God may not be destroyed, but be preserved by warning and be consoled."[108]

Dirk Philips, one of the most influential Dutch Anabaptists in the early decades of the movement, writes explicitly about the calling or sending of teachers, ministers, and missionaries, identifying two kinds of calling "to an office" that are included in Scripture. One of those callings is from God alone, as in the case of Moses or Aaron or some of the prophets, without mediation from others. The other kind of calling, says Philips, is both from God and from God's congregations.

The point of Philips' words is that teachers and ministers in the church do not call themselves but are "called, chose[n], and ordained" by God or God's congregation. The Holy Spirit, says Philips, will touch new ministers' hearts, making them "fiery with love" to "voluntarily feed, lead, and send out the congregation of God."[109]

CHOOSING PASTORS BY LOT

Many of the early Anabaptists, of course, and their ancestors in later centuries, have chosen their pastors by lot. Hutterite Peter Riedemann says members should not elect ministers to please themselves but should "wait on the Lord to see whom he chooses and indicates."[110]

Among more conservative Mennonites, part of the stream out of which those from Mennonite Church backgrounds come, both church architecture and leader selection processes have evidenced shared ministry within the body of Christ. Pulpits on a raised platform suggested proud leadership, it was believed, and were more appropriate for an educated, professional, Protestant clergy than for humble Mennonite leaders. Mennonite historian James C. Juhnke writes about nineteenth and early twentieth-century leaders among the more theologically conservative Mennonite groups:

Like Christ, Mennonite leaders were supposed to be servants. Ministers had no professional training nor were they paid. Young Mennonite men with genuine leadership potential were expected to have the virtues of humility and self-effacement rather than to claim a personal "call" or a gift for aggressive leadership. No aspiring minister would openly seek the burden of leading the church. Congregations chose ministers by "lot," a process which protected them against the consolidation of power which comes when leaders choose their own successors.[111]

The process of selecting by lot included having potential leaders choose from a number of Bibles; the one who chose the Bible with a special verse inserted in the text was the one chosen by God, it was believed.

In an article addressing the practice of choosing ministers by lot, Mennonite Church USA leader Ervin Stutzman speaks extensively about the German concept of *Gelassenheit*, the "shared yieldedness" that related both to the congregation practicing the lot and to the ministers chosen or overlooked in the process.

Part of the purpose of the lot was to keep potential ministers from striving after the position, or from "forwardness." Among the spiritual benefits of choosing ministers by lot, says Stutzman, were reflecting the spiritual values of yieldedness, humility, and community, as well as the power of the climactic moment of choosing the appropriate Bible, which seemingly conferred God's blessing. Selecting ministers by lot also provided Mennonite churches with an ever-ready supply of ministers.[112]

The *Mennonite Polity for Ministerial Leadership*, a manual for pastors edited by church journalist Everett J. Thomas, does an excellent job of more thoroughly tracing out "Ministry and Mennonite History." It is recommended for those wanting an overview of the development of Mennonites' perspectives on ministry in the church.

The polity document affirms the ministry of all baptized believers and also affirms calling out particular people for ministerial offices. The latter are those who are called to long-term service in facilitating and equipping the church's ministry, serving as representatives of a local congregation or the church body as a whole, with particular responsibility for community leadership and oversight.[113] For contemporary Mennonites and their Anabaptist forebears, serving in ministerial offices has come to mean experiencing both an "outer call" from the body of believers and an "inner call" through one's own prayer, reflection, recognition of gifts, and commitments.[114]

THE PRIESTHOOD OF ALL BELIEVERS

As already suggested, from the sixteenth century to today, Mennonites have had diverse and contested views about pastoral ministry, including how much authority should be given to called-out pastors and what the meaning and status of ordination is in a church that embraces a "priesthood of all believers."

In its original Protestant form, the concept of "priesthood of all believers" referred largely to not needing a mediator between believers and God—to not needing a professional priest to intercede for believers. Believers have direct access to God, the concept implies. The "priesthood of all believers" also suggests, as was emphasized in the 1960s and thereafter among some U.S. Mennonites, the idea that "everyone is equally a leader" in the church.

Ambivalence about pastoral ministry was present throughout twentieth-century Mennonite developments in pastoral ministry—from the shift away from bivocational, self-supported pastors toward paid, professional, increasingly educated ministers; through the 1960s and 1970s shift away from pastoral authoritarianism and toward shared leadership that denied a place for pastoral positions; through the early and present years regarding women's involvement in ministry; and through the more general debates about the validity of ordination, given that ordination is an extra-biblical practice in a faith tradition that prides itself in a biblically based understanding of the church.

In the Mennonite church, providing salaries to pastors was met initially with stiff resistance in the early and mid-twentieth century,[115] with self-supporting Mennonite ministers sometimes looking down on their paid peers. More recently some salaried, seminary-trained Mennonite pastors have likewise denigrated their untrained, bivocational peers. Some have perceived that the church's egalitarian approach of the 1960s and beyond "has not served us well," allowing pastoral leaders to fulfill certain tasks or functions but lacking any understanding of pastoral positions or responsibilities. "Concepts about shared leadership," says John A. Esau, "tended to degenerate into meaning that the pastor lost the power and authority required to serve the church effectively."[116]

Adding to the ambivalence regarding pastoral ministry is the occasional power *denial* of those in ministry, a denial that on occasion has contributed to sexual and other power abuses. Regarding ordination,[117] biblical scholar Dorothy Yoder Nyce has been one of the most outspoken critics of the practice, urging an end to "the selective rite of ordination" which "abort[s]" the authentic priesthood of all believers.[118] Yoder Nyce believes that Jesus' baptism of water and the Spirit—a baptism shared by believers since his day—was his "ordination" for his leading, healing, calling, and forgiving ministries.

In theologian John Howard Yoder's[119] view, the role of the "professional religionist," a role that develops in nearly all societies from the most primitive to the most modern, is part of the fallen nature of humanity, not God's intention. No one should have monopoly on access to the divine. Jesus instead "formed a movement out of fishermen, zealots, and publicans—and women," says Yoder. "The specialized purveyor of access to the divine is out of work since Pentecost."[120]

All members of the body of Christ are given ministerial roles; moreover, those roles least justified by Christian Scriptures, says Yoder, are those of priest and bishop. Regarding these various ministries in the church, Yoder writes, "The transformation that Paul's vision calls for . . . would be to reorient the notion of ministry so that there would be no one ungifted, no one not called, no one not empowered, and no one dominated."[121]

Current Mennonite polity seeks to address these concerns, acknowledging the ministry of all within the church but still supporting calling out some to be designated leaders in the offices of ministry, and ordaining those with such a calling for their work. Ordination is perceived in the *Mennonite Polity* document as an act of a congregation, conference, and denomination to call and appoint a member "to ongoing leadership ministry in the life and mission of the church."[122]

Likely the ambivalence some Mennonites feel about ordination and other aspects of ministry will continue, stimulating additional, essential conversations rooted in and reflecting historic Anabaptist tensions regarding the role of leaders in the church. But as we will suggest in Chapter 9, it is good to designate and call out certain people for pastoral roles in our congregations.

QUESTIONS FOR REFLECTION

1. Can you identify what the Anabaptists' concerns were about priests and pastors? Are these concerns relevant at all in a twenty-first-century world?

2. What was the intention of choosing pastors by "lot," and what do you think of such a system of identifying leaders? What would be some of the concerns with choosing pastors this way?

3. What special gifts do congregational pastors need in today's world? In the class or small group you are meeting with, who would you identify as a possible future pastor?

4. Has anyone ever suggested that you should consider

pastoral ministry or some other form of church leadership? How have you responded, if so? Do you feel any sort of inner calling to church leadership?

5. Do you believe the church should ordain people who are called to pastoral leadership? Why or why not? Is this a biblical practice? Should all members of a church consider their baptism their ordination into Christ's service? What are the benefits of identifying some particular called-out church leaders?

6. How have you understood the concept of "the priesthood of all believers"? For you, what does the concept suggest about leadership in the church?

Chapter 8

GUIDING DISCIPLES

Clearly, North American Mennonites and other Christians in the twenty-first century live in a very different context than that of their spiritual ancestors. Mennonites and other Christians—at least in North America—are not persecuted for their faith, nor do they need to provide theological arguments for a posture of withdrawal that was once necessary for their survival. The view of the church as a voluntary organization, separated from the state's rule—a radical Anabaptist view in the sixteenth century—is now commonplace for Christians of all stripes. And though many Mennonites continue to have suspicions about denominational hierarchies, they no longer share the anticlericalism of their ancestors.

Today Mennonites have full access to professions from which they were previously barred. They are moving eagerly into these occupations and others that simply did not exist in earlier centuries.

At the same time, sixteenth-century Anabaptists and twenty-first-century North American Mennonites do share some theological and ethical continuity in terms of their vocational experience. What the Anabaptists wanted to do, explicitly and implicitly, was recapture the sense that being a Christian shaped—and even transformed—every aspect of life. They fully embraced Paul's assertion to the church at Corinth:

> So if anyone is in Christ, there is a new creation: everything old has passed away; see, everything has become new! All this is from God, who reconciled us to himself through Christ, and has given us the ministry of reconciliation. (2 Cor. 5:17-18)

In the past, verse 17 was often translated as, "If anyone is in Christ, he or she is a new creature," which suggests just an inner transformation of the person. More recent biblical scholars have suggested that what Paul is saying is really more like what is said above: "If anyone is in Christ, new is creation," or "there is a whole new world." The focus, then, is not so much on changing our being but on completely transforming the perspective of those who accept Christ as their life context.[123] What we once viewed quite differently, what we may have seen once as useless scraps, we come to see as full of potential, components woven or sewn into a beautiful new creation all around us and within us.

I often credit my spouse Ann with teaching me how to see. She's an artist, a watercolorist, and a designer, and she was raised to view the world through an artist's eyes. Where I once saw a gray lake I now see gradations of purples, whites, blues, and shimmering reflections of trees in the ripples. Where I once saw a yellow flower I now see sunlight manipulating angles and shadows, playfully illuminating petals and leaves. There is a whole new world.

Contemporary Mennonites desire nothing less, even as they recognize the complexity of bringing these convictions to bear in the context of modern life.

What follows in this and the final chapter are six basic points of continuity within the Anabaptist-Mennonite tradition that offer a framework for future conversations regarding a contemporary Christian theology of vocation from a Mennonite perspective.

1. Calling should be understood primarily and fundamentally as being a follower of Jesus Christ.

When asked about his vocation, an early Anabaptist reportedly said, "My vocation is to follow Christ. To make a living I am a tailor."[124] This is similar to the larger Protestant notion of a "general" as opposed to a "particular" calling,[125] but that broader sense of vocation has carried more weight within an Anabaptist-Mennonite ethical framework. For Anabaptists, the Christian's essential vocation is to live faithfully—to recognize that the claim to be a follower of Jesus changes them and their perspective on the world. Calling is best understood simply as following Christ: Our true vocation, no matter what our particular work, is Christian discipleship.

Such a calling to discipleship is not just about professions and paid work but shapes how Mennonite Christians engage in relationships, how they spend their free time, how they form and keep and relate to families, whether or not they choose to have children, how they parent, how they make decisions about money, how they open themselves to others who are different, and how they serve others. Especially amid warfare in oil-rich countries around the world, Mennonites should be conscious of what they consume and the ways in which that consumption serves to justify nations' perceived need to make wars. Faith communities, congregations, and denominations may also have collective vocations to offer a distinctive contribution to God's world.

2. A Christian theology of vocation in Mennonite perspective honors and blesses the ways followers of Jesus live out their faith in their occupational, professional, and worldly roles.

Mennonites and other Christians need to keep working out the relationship between what they do in church and what they do as church in their lives. "Being the church" includes being scattered into various places of employment within society's institutions. These locations will likely include not only teaching, health care, and social services but also professional engagement in political and economic life. The church can be the church in various voluntary organizations working to change society, in justice-conscious businesses, in creative work of many types, and even in public office when one's work is geared toward serving God and the common good.[126] "Being church" ought to penetrate these work-a-day worlds.

However, Mennonite Christians should be reluctant to call their paid work their "vocation," since such a view misunderstands biblical perspectives on calling and truncates the broader notion of vocation. Most North Americans move in and out of various occupations over the course of a lifetime, often significantly changing jobs every five to seven years. Referring to each of these specific positions as "callings" would seem odd.

At the same time, it is clear that our practices in our work-a-day worlds are more nuanced, complicated, and contradictory than what is sometimes described above. That is partly because Christians are called not just to be Christians "in general," but to be Christians in concrete locations—as friends, as spouses, as parents, as citizens, and as laborers and professionals.

The "general call" of Christ takes specific form: "as a prism refracts light into a variety of colors, so too one's relational setting refracts God's general call" into a variety of settings, says Lutheran scholar Douglas Schuurman.[127] Christians express their faith in and often through organizational and institutional and relational structures, including at the places where they work.[128] As such, the church should bless those who serve the cause of Christ in their various, flexible, ever-changing "stations" in life.[129]

3. A commitment to being Jesus' disciples ought to shape and transform occupational, business, and professional roles. In its ideal form, the call to discipleship drives paid work more than the typical demands of the role or the occupation itself.

When vocation is rooted in discipleship, vocation is about more than making occupational and educational choices; it is also about what sustains and nurtures Christians in those roles. What keeps Christians faithful to their primary vocation as Christ's disciples? Thus, it might be ethically sensitive for Mennonites to identify themselves with the qualifier "Mennonite," as in Mennonite lawyer, Mennonite teacher, Mennonite physician, Mennonite businessperson, Mennonite factory worker, or Mennonite farmer, simply as a reminder of the call to discipleship.[130] Other Christians might choose to do the same with their own denominational adjectives or with the modifier *Christian* before their occupation.

When Mennonites began entering various professions in great numbers in the 1960s and 1970s, several organizations sprang up to walk alongside those church members who had chosen fields previously disdained. Those organizations—especially groups for lawyers and for businesspeople—helped Mennonites think about their work, challenge each other to be faithful to their Christian callings, and to live against the grain when necessary. Some of those organizations have now ceased to exist, but there would be great value in resurrecting such communal structures to help Mennonites think carefully about their work.

Mennonites and other Christians in business ought not be doing what all other business people do. Mennonite lawyers and physicians ought to think about their fee structures and their practices in ways that do not fully parallel those of their colleagues. Mennonite professors ought to stand with one foot in the academy and one foot firmly lodged in the church. As Mennonite theologian John H. Yoder has written,

> If we reclaim the doctrine of vocation in the light of [our tradition's] practices and social vision . . . then the specific ministry of the Christian banker or financier will be to find realistic, technically not utopian ways of implementing jubilee amnesty;

there are people doing this. The Christian realtor or developer will find ways to house people according to need; there are people doing this. The Christian judge will open the court system to conflict resolution procedures, and resist the trend toward more and more litigation; this is being done. Technical vocational sphere expertise in each professional area will be needed not to reinforce but to undercut competently the claimed sovereignty of each sphere by planting signs of the new world in the ruins of the old.[131]

Mennonites and other Christians should enter professions and business with a "strategy of creative subversion," with only partial loyalty to the demands of their roles and a willingness to think critically about the demands of those roles.[132]

Faithful Christians will not necessarily do what any other reasonable person would do in their occupational role. Instead, as Yoder argues, they need to be "judged and renewed by the difference it makes that Christ, and not mammon or mars, is their Lord."[133] Christians should be visible in their civic communities and workplaces, keeping their promises, loving their enemies, telling the truth, and enjoying their neighbors. Such behavior, says Yoder, "may communicate something of the reconciling, i.e., the community-creating, love of God."[134]

In today's world, so governed by multinational corporations and the military-industrial complex, transformation and creative subversion may be a twenty-first-century form of Mennonite "conscientious objection,"[135] an economic moral equivalent to Mennonites' age-old response to warfare.

When Christians find themselves in work that constrains the expression of their discipleship, for example, or that calls them to contribute to brokenness rather than healing, to strife rather than reconciliation, to exploitation rather than nurture, they should leave that place of work and express their vocation as disciples elsewhere.[136] Because of the difficulty of engaging in "vocational conscientious objection," congregational accountability is essential. In today's world, here is where Christians may most need their sisters and brothers in the church to keep each other accountable to their commitments of fidelity to Christ and Christian discipleship.

In the final chapter we'll look at three more guiding principles, but these represent a good place to start when thinking faithfully about God's callings on our lives.

QUESTIONS FOR REFLECTION

1. Does it makes sense to think about Christian calling and vocation as primarily Christian discipleship?

2. Do you agree or disagree with the author's three main assertions in this chapter? How would you nuance or change what the author says?

3. If compromise and accommodation are essential in some occupations or professions, how does the faithful Christian know when she or he has gone too far? If you have a good bit of life/work experience, do you have any stories that show where compromise and accommodation are essential?

4. In what ways do the products of our labor contribute to the spreading of violence around the world, and is this acceptable?

5. With sisters and brothers in the church, are you willing to "give and receive counsel" regarding vocational choices?

6. In your present or future work, how can you imagine your calling to Christian discipleship altering what you do in that occupation or profession?

Chapter 9

HONORING LEADERS, SEEKING HEALING

In Chapter 8 we identified three initial principles for guiding faithful Christians as they reflect on and embrace their vocations: 1) seeing faithful discipleship as our primary calling; 2) honoring and blessing the way followers of Jesus live out their faith in their occupational, professional, and worldly roles; and 3) allowing our commitments to being Jesus' disciples to shape and transform our roles. In this final chapter we look at three additional guidelines for embracing vocation in the contemporary world.

1. A Christian theology of vocation in a Mennonite perspective should honor the place of called-out leaders in the church.

Given the significance of the church as the locus for nurturing Christians in faith, leading them in modeling God's reign, and sending them as disciples into the world, congregations should be guided by leaders who are empowered and blessed to lead. As earlier noted, John H. Yoder has described the role of the "professional religionist" as part of the fallen nature of humanity outside of God's intention, noting that all members of the body of

Christ are given ministerial roles, with no one having a monopoly on access to the divine.[137]

However, often the hesitance to honor called-out leaders in the church comes from the mistaken assumption of the "scarcity of affirmation"—the belief that there is only so much affirmation to go around.[138] There should be an abundance of affirmation in the church: for paid, professional leaders; for maintenance staff; for Sunday school teachers; for elders; for those who create art and lead music; for those who practice hospitality. The church at its best should honor each of these roles and then still have more affirmation to go around.

The church—including congregations, districts, conferences, denominations, and church schools—should actively, energetically, and passionately call the brightest and best and most faithful of its young people into Christian leadership roles.[139] Parents should introduce the possibility of Christian ministry to their children in their early years, and congregations should tap young people on their shoulders in their adolescent and teen years.

Both women and men should be invited to consider pastoral ministry and provided with the counsel and resources needed to discern that inner and outer calling. The issue is not only needing to fill our pulpits and parsonages but being faithful in drawing those with ministering gifts into service in the church.

As earlier discussed, whether or not such "honoring" should include the extra-biblical practice of ordination remains open to debate within contemporary Mennonite circles. Certainly the transformation of work-a-day roles for Mennonites in the professions also includes transformation of pastoral ministry. Pastors in the Anabaptist-Mennonite tradition should have a keen sense of shared leadership. They should recognize their role as visionary and authoritative but not authoritarian leaders. They should function as facilitators, drawing out the many spiritual gifts of others in the congregation. And they should live with authenticity and integrity, with an egalitarian spirit, and with honorable relationships, modeling for others faithful discipleship.

2. God's callings may not always line up with our initial hopes, expectations, or particular occupational preparation.

Throughout Hebrew Scriptures, those who receive direct calls from God are almost never expecting the calls, and they meet them with resistance and rejection rather than warm acceptance. Even Isaiah's enthusiastic "Here I am; send me!" (Isa. 6:8) is countered by his protests once he finds out what God is calling him to do. To be sustained in long-term work, however, Christians need to have a sense that they are using their abilities in ways that serve God's purposes. They then need to embrace that location, continue preparation for their work, and develop systems of support and accountability. In time, they need to discover true joy in their particular settings if their work is to be life-giving for themselves and others.

When former Mennonite Central Committee Executive Secretary Robb Davis spoke at Goshen College a few years ago, he urged students to pursue their passions and then to link those passions with Christ's mission on earth.[140] Davis used the simple yet profound illustration of a mosquito net to talk about callings. Mosquito nets in malaria-debilitated parts of Africa would save thousands of lives. Davis encouraged Goshen's students with passions in the natural sciences to develop new and better ways of producing such nets; those with technical skills to develop more efficient means of manufacturing the nets; those with marketing desires to think about the best ways to package the nets so they can be safely shipped to where they need to go; those with teaching skills to consider working in Africa to educate others about the value and proper use of mosquito nets for their health; and those with a passion for social justice or politics to press their government leaders to help with the production and distribution of such nets. Davis said students should pursue their passions and link them with Christ's mission in the world.

In a complex economic world, some people are compelled, over the course of an entire lifetime, to work in locations where they find no passion or joy, where their vocational souls are sucked out in repetitive and relatively meaningless tasks. Sometimes this is referred to as "making a living," but Mennonites and other Christians ought to seek for themselves and for others humane systems and workplaces where all can not only "make a living88

" but "make a life." That is to say, we should seek lives that are integrated, where work flows out of who we are and allows us to express our faith through relationships, our interactions with friends and strangers, an attentiveness to the creative products of our labor, and the use of our natural and schooled gifts and abilities.[141]

3. The primary content of our vocation as disciples of Jesus Christ is to work at bringing healing and reconciliation in God's good and groaning world.

When, in Luke 4, Jesus announces his own mission and calling in his hometown of Nazareth, he describes it in Jubilee language from the lectionary text in Isaiah 61—to bring good news to the poor, to proclaim release to the captives and recovery of sight to the blind, to let the oppressed go free, to proclaim the year of the Lord's favor (Luke 4:18-19).

Shortly before their deaths, Atlee and Winifred Beechy, who committed their lives to service at Goshen College and with Mennonite Central Committee in Europe, Vietnam, China, and elsewhere, sent out a Christmas letter that encouraged recipients to "relax and rejoice in the coming of God's son and in God's amazing and unrationed grace that calls us into Christ's ministry of reconciliation."

"Our vocation," they wrote,

> is to praise and serve God; share God's transforming grace; keep hope alive; invite people to become reconciled to God, to each other, and to themselves; and to share God's freeing nonviolent alternative

that transforms enemies into friends.

"We want to do this," Atlee and Winnie continued,

not with self-righteous piety or a distorted sense of duty, but with love, humility, hope, humor, and grace-filled hearts. We invite you to join us in responding to this continuing challenge.

Twenty-first-century Mennonites and other Christians who are committed to faithful vocations will need eyes to see clearly, ears to hear precisely, hearts to embrace lovingly, and spirits to commit joyfully, alongside others, to God's ministry of embrace and reconciliation: mending the brokenness, bringing together those who have only known enmity, and proclaiming Christ's radical vision of social transformation that will prevent future brokenness from occurring.

MENDING THE WORLD'S BROKENNESS

Some years ago, while a graduate student in religion at Harvard University, Mary Moschella gave Harvard's baccalaureate address. In the speech, she notes that she and her colleagues were drawn to the university because of the "modest desire to learn to see everything clearly." She observes that "We came to explore the very mysteries of God, to expand our view of the world, and to discern what it is that the universe demands of us."

And then Moschella tells a story about the summer she spent working on an archaeological dig in Israel, a tale that speaks eloquently about learning to see anew, and discovering a vocation. She describes swinging her pick into the soil at the ancient city of Dor as, symbolically, a way of working out her own faith and belief. While working, she often found herself "cursing the facts of human suffering in the world, and trying to imagine some kind of hope of restoration," she says.

As is true of many archaeological digs, Moschella and her fellow workers only occasionally uncovered pottery shards, and never in her square that season did she recover a single whole vessel—"just so many broken pieces, scraps of ancient civilization," she says, a reality that came to function as a "metaphor for understanding the world." The world, too, is broken, observes Moschella, both with "small personal pains" and "overwhelmingly large human struggles."

But Moschella went through her own transformation as the summer continued and she kept studying the pottery shards. She reports beginning to notice that, though broken, some of the clay pieces were extraordinarily beautiful. Shortly thereafter she learned about the process of mending pottery. "Seeing those restored vessels," she notes, "encouraged me to imagine perhaps that at least some of the world's brokenness could be overcome." She reports that she began to see herself in the "vocation of mending, repairing some of the world's brokenness" and "proclaim[ing] a radical vision of social transformation that would prevent future brokenness from occurring."[142]

If anyone is in Christ, there is a new creation. May we begin to see how God might use our gifts and our work to further God's desires for our world.

QUESTIONS FOR REFLECTION

1. What do you think about the concept of an "abundance of affirmation" rather than a "scarcity of affirmation" in the church? Is this the way you've seen the church practicing its affirmation of church members and leaders?

2. How are "making a living" and "making a life" different from each other?

3. What do you see as Jesus' primary mission and message? Here the author argues that we can find Jesus' own understanding in the Luke 4 passage. Would you agree or disagree with that, and why?

4. In the Jewish tradition, the Hebrew phrase *tikkun olam*, which means "repairing the world," has become a significant theme connoting social action, community

service, and social justice. In what ways do you think you might repair some of the world's brokenness?

5. How have your perceptions of vocation changed as you have gone through this study? How have they remained the same?

6. Who in your group would you like to affirm, and for what gifts? What gifts do you hope others see in you?

EPILOGUE: MATTERING LIVES

I began this book with a story about my father-in-law and his Brethren Service Committee trip to Poland after World War II. Some fifty years after Ron's post-war service on the horse boat, an Eastern European man visited Ron and Esther at their home in the hills near Aibonito, Puerto Rico. The visitor was a financial consultant based in San Juan and was helping them set up their retirement plan.

While talking with Esther and Ron, the consultant noticed over the fireplace a metal plaque with the words "Danziger Feuersocietät." As a seventeen-year-old, Ron had picked up the fire station marker from out of the rubble of a bombed Danzig street. Ron explained to the visitor that before he went to college he went with Brethren Service Committee to take horses to Poland, distributing work-horses to people in need.

And the face of the visitor from half a world away—a visitor who had come to their Aibonito home to serve them—began to tremble. With tears in his eyes, he said, "Our family received one of those horses. It was all that we had, and it's the only reason we were able to survive through that winter."[143]

Service to others, in the spirit of Christ, makes a difference in our world, and calls us toward our true vocation as disciples of Christ. Just as we have been reconciled to God through Christ, we have been given—entrusted with—the ministry of reconciliation to others. The vision for the church and for all of us

> is a vision of reconciliation of all things—the creation of a dynamic harmony in a world ravaged by life-impairing strife. To live and preach the gospel means to help make this grand vision of reconciliation a reality.[144]

NOTES

1. This story is told in Ronald Graber and Esther Rose Graber, "The Retrospectroscope," an unpublished speech given upon their receipt of Goshen College's "Culture for Service" award in October 2003. Available from the author.

2. Frederick Buechner, in an oft-quoted aphorism, wrote that "The place God calls you is the place where your deep gladness and the world's deep hunger meet." Frederick Buechner, *Wishful Thinking: A Seeker's ABC* (San Francisco: HarperSanFrancisco, 1993), 119.

3. David Guterson, *East of the Mountains* (San Diego: Harcourt, Inc., 2000).

4. Guterson, *East of the Mountains*.

5. Douglas J. Schuurman, *Vocation: Discerning Our Callings in Life* (Grand Rapids: William B. Eerdmans Publishing Company, 2004), xiii. He notes that when many people talk about vocational training or vocational schools or "choosing a vocation," they are thinking quite narrowly about a career or a technical field. Schuurman writes: "Constructive treatments of vocation for the past few decades constrict the idea to paid work, neglecting the potential of vocation to integrate paid and unpaid work, domestic and 'public' life, church and world, personal identity and varied roles, faith and life. The way vocation has become synonymous with paid work—even within theological treatments—expresses the sad state of affairs in which an originally

expansive concept has become tidily constricted (and conscripted) in modern life." Later, on p. 2, Schuurman notes that while "calling" and "vocation" are synonymous for most Protestants, the former term appears to be less secularized and restricted to paid work than the latter term. On distinctions between occupations, professions, and callings, see also Calvin Redekop and Urie A. Bender, *Who Am I? What Am I? Searching for Meaning in Your Work* (Grand Rapids: Academie Books, 1988), 221-222.

6. Douglas J. Schuurman, *Vocation*, loc. cit., 18. Schuurman also says that among the Hebrew terms sometimes translated as "call" is *qahal*, a reference to the people God calls together for service. This is an overstatement of the Hebrew use of the term, and is based more on an anachronistic "reading back" of the Greek term *ekklesia* into the Hebrew *qahal*. The latter term really does not connote this sense of "called out."

7. Douglas J. Schuurman, *Vocation*, loc. cit., 17. Among the Hebrew terms Schuurman identifies, p. 18, that speak to this first form of calling is the verb *qara'*, which means "to call," and is often associated with *bahar*, meaning "election."

8. Joyce Ann Mercer identifies this difference as Calling with a capital "C" (the general calling) and calling with a lower case "c"—the specific locations where we "witness to God's saving grace in our lives." See Joyce Ann Mercer, "Are We Going on a Vocation Now? Ministry with Youth as a Lifelong Passion," in Amy Scott Vaugh, editor, *Compass Points: Navigating Vocation: The 2002 Princeton Lectures on Youth, Church, and Culture* (Princeton, New Jersey: Princeton Theological Seminary, 2002), 49. Mennonite philosopher and administrator J. Lawrence Burkholder wrote in his early years of teaching, "If we were to rediscover the New Testament doctrine of work in relation to the Great Commission, it would revolutionize the church in a single generation. It would mean that Christians would consider mission work and Christian social service as a natural calling rather than a special calling. It would mean that every Christian young person would prepare for the future in the light of the call of the church." See J. Lawrence Burkholder, *Church and Community*, 9. Cited in Virgil Vogt, *The Christian Calling* (Scottdale, Pa.: Mennonite Publishing House, 1961), 41-42.

9. Paul Marshall, *A Kind of Life*, loc. cit., 14.

10. Rupert Davies, "Vocation," in *The Westminster Dictionary of Christian Theology*, ed. Alan Richardson and John Bowden

(Philadelphia: Westminster Press, 1983), 601.

11. On this, see, e.g., Mary Jo Weaver, *Introduction to Christianity*, 3rd. ed. (Belmont, Calif.: Wadsworth Publishing Company, 1998), 63-66. Weaver identifies four different forms of third- and fourth-century monasticism, each practiced by both men and women. Apotactic monks were the earliest monks, and their form of monasticism was practiced particularly by women. They were those who "lived in cities, worshiped in parish churches, and sometimes had jobs, but they followed an ascetic discipline of celibacy, fasting, and simplicity in dress." Eremetic monks, also known as hermits, lived by themselves in the desert and had only occasional contact with other people. Semi-eretic monks "were hermits who lived in dwellings within shouting distance of other hermits," meeting weekly for shared worship and a meal. Coenobitic monks lived together in monasteries and "followed a regular routine of prayer, study, and physical labor set down in a rule." Most contemporary monks are coenobitic monks.

12. The fourth-century church father Eusebius writes, "Two ways of life were thus given by the law of Christ to His Church. The one is above nature, and beyond common human living ... permanently separate from the common customary life of [humanity], it devotes itself to the service of God alone .... Such then is the perfect form of the Christian life." The other form of Christian life, says Eusebius, is "more humble, more human, permits man to join in pure nuptials, and to produce children ... it allows them to have minds for farming, for trade, and the other more secular interests as well as for religion ... a kind of secondary grade of piety is attributed to them." See J.B. Lightfoot, editor, *The Apostolic Fathers* (London: Macmillan, 1926), 487-511. Cited in Paul Marshall, *A Kind of Life*, loc. cit., 18-19.

13. Douglas J. Schuurman, *Vocation*, loc. cit., 2. Schuurman notes that while the *Catholic Encyclopedia* completely omits reference to non-ecclesial forms of vocation, the *Cathechism of the Catholic Church* (2nd. ed.), has a more expansive view that includes the "vocation of lay people" in a way that would lead "Calvin or Luther [to] respond to these words with a hearty 'Amen!'"

14. One example of this is Marie Theresa Coombs and Francis Kelly Nemeck, *Called by God: A Theology of Vocation and Lifelong*

Commitment (Eugene, Oregon: Wipf and Stock, Publishers, 2001). Originally published in 1992, the text by these two religious Catholics, one a hermit and one a monk, focuses almost entirely on traditionally understood religious vocations, though it also addresses the question of marriage as a vocation.

15. These opening sentences are paraphrased, in slightly different order and form, from Rupert Davies, "Vocation," loc. cit., 601.

16. Becky Bontrager Horst called this story to my attention. An online version of it can be found at www.naute.com/stories /3stonecutters.php

17. Martin Luther, *Day by Day We Magnify Thee* (Philadelphia: Fortress Press, 1982), 298.

18. John Dillenberger, in *Martin Luther: Selections from His Writings* (New York: Anchor Press, 1961), writes: "When Luther denied that monasticism was a higher calling than the other stations in [people's] lives, the foundation for monasticism collapsed in many sections of Germany, and the Reformation faced the problem of the rehabilitation of countless monks and nuns who were fleeing the monasteries, as well as the difficult task of reconceiving the whole understanding of Christian vocation." One of the fleeing nuns, Katharine von Bora, would settle for nothing less than marrying Luther himself.

19. Max Weber, *The Protestant Ethic*, loc. cit., 80.

20. The inclusion of "Christian" here is important in Luther's thought. Although non-Christians have station (*Stand*) and office (*Amt*), *Beruf* is specifically the Christian's earthly or spiritual work. On this, see Gustaf Wingren, *Luther on Vocation*, loc. cit., 2.

21. See Paul Althaus, *Ethics of Martin Luther*, translated by R.C. Schultz (Philadelphia: Muhlenberg Press, 1972), 36ff.; and Martin Luther, *Luther's Works*, (55 volumes), 14:15 and 13:369, edited by Jaroslav Pelikan; and 46:246, edited by H.T. Lehmann (Philadelphia and St. Louis: Concordia and Muhlenberg Press), 1955-1986. Cited in Paul Marshall, *A Kind of Life*, loc. cit., 14.

22. Paul Marshall, *A Kind of Life*, loc. cit., 23. *Stand* has the meaning of particular orders of society such as state, family, economy, or church. *Amt* is one's office, what one does in a particular *Stand*.

23. On this, see Paul Marshall, *A Kind of Life*, loc. cit., 24.

24. John Calvin, *Institutes of the Christian Religion*, Book III:10,

ed. John T. McNeill, translated and ed. Ford Lewis Battles (Philadelphia: Westminster Press, 1960), 724.

25. Cited in Gustaf Wingren, *Luther on Vocation*, loc. cit., 88. In *The Protestant Ethic*, 84-85, Max Weber argues that Luther's initial conservatism in this regard was rooted in Paul's apparent indifference about worldly activity. Passages such as I Corinthians 7:17, which is about singleness or marriage, suggest that Christians should "lead the life that the Lord has assigned, to which God called you," partly because of early Christians' eschatological expectations about Jesus' imminent return. Over time, though, says Weber, Luther's conservatism was rooted in a stronger, more intense belief in divine providence, "which identified absolute obedience to God's will, with absolute acceptance of things as they were." In a similar vein, John Calvin writes that each person "will bear and swallow the discomforts, vexations, weariness, and anxieties in his [or her] way of life, when he [or she] has been persuaded that the burden was laid upon him [or her] by God. From this will arise also a singular consolation: that no task will be so sordid and base, provided you obey your calling in it, that it will not shine and be reckoned very precious in God's sight." See John Calvin, *Institutes*, loc. cit., 725.

26. See G. Harkness, *John Calvin: The Man and His Ethics* (New York: Holt, 1931), 212. See also Calvin's essay titled "On What the Libertines Understand by the Vocation of Believers, and How Under This Guise They Excuse Every Form of Villainy," in B.W. Farley, editor and translator, *John Calvin: Treatises Against the Anabaptists and Against the Libertines* (Grand Rapids: Baker Books, 1988).

27. Paul Marshall, *A Kind of Life*, loc. cit., 25. Marshall also notes in this context that Calvin altered the understanding of "talents" in the biblical story of the talents of gold (Matthew 25:14-30). Marshall writes: "Before Calvin the talents of gold, which one should use to glorify God, were seen as spiritual gifts and graces that God had bestowed on Christians. Calvin made a revolutionary change in interpretation when he understood the talents in terms of one's calling and in terms of people's 'talents.'"

28. John H. Yoder, a critic of such views, writes, in *The Royal Priesthood: Essays Ecclesiological and Ecumenical*, ed. Michael G. Cartwright (Grand Rapids: Eerdmans, 1994), 95, that, "In mod-

ern parlance, 'public service' has become the standard euphe-
mism for the exercise of power, thus fulfilling in the name of the
'Christian calling' what Jesus ironically said about pagan rulers,
namely that they glorify the exercise of power over people as
'benefaction.'" On this, see Luke 22:25-26 and Matthew 20:25.

29. Martin Luther, "The Sermon on the Mount," translated
and edited by Jaroslav Pelikan, in *Luther's Works*, Vol. 21 (St.
Louis: Concordia Publishing House, 1956), 37. In "Whether
Soldiers, Too, Can Be Saved," Luther writes: "It is not [humans],
but God, who hangs, tortures, beheads, kills, and fights. All
these are God's works and judgments." See Martin Luther,
Luther's Works, Vol. 46, ed. by Robert C. Schultz (Philadelphia:
Fortress Press, 1967), 96. I am conscious that in selecting these
passages I am drawing out some of the more controversial
aspects of Luther's teaching on vocation. Our Anabaptist forebears latched onto these teachings, however, and understanding these tensions helps set the stage for Anabaptist critiques of
Luther's view.

30. Gustaf Wingren, *Luther on Vocation*, loc. cit., 178-179.

31. Douglas J. Schuurman, a contemporary interpreter and
defender of the Protestant view of vocation, rightly understood,
also notes some contemporary critiques of Protestant versions
of vocation. He recognizes in *Vocation*, p. 13, that in terms of
paid work, "economic forces have eclipsed the role vocation
used to play in shaping relations between employer and
employee, between business and community." Vocation, he
says, "generates loyalty, mutual trust, and concern for the larger, long-term ends of an occupation. These qualities are exceedingly difficult to sustain in today's bureaucratic context." Bereft
of the formative effect of vocation in work relationships, the
doctrine of vocation faces "many pitfalls, and it can be and has
been misused to exploitative and oppressive ends," Schuurman
writes on p. 15. "The doctrine of vocation is blamed for engen-
dering and sustaining oppression. Marxists have long condemned the ways in which the rich and powerful use the idea
of vocation to keep economically oppressed people from challenging those who oppress them. Liberals suggest that the concept of vocation has perpetuated inequalities in economic
opportunity and remuneration by encouraging ascription (by
arguing, for example, that women's vocation is domestic) and
by justifying lower-than-normal wages (since it is a vocation to

teach at a religious institution, one should not press authorities for higher wages). More recently feminists perceive in the idea of vocation an affirmation of a hierarchical understanding of human nature, society, and God. The effect of vocation is thought to inhibit moral agency and autonomy by encouraging 'obedience' to the 'summons' of the Divine Commander. In the minds of many, vocation smacks of a conservative quietism in its religious interpretation of authority and, insofar as the reformist or revolutionary spirit of the modern West is at odds with conservatism, this spirit condemns conservatism's alleged ally, vocation." In spite of these possible pitfalls, Schuurman argues convincingly that vocation "remains a vital source of wisdom about faithful Christian living in the modern world."

32. John H. Yoder, *Body Politics: Five Practices of the Christian Community Before the Watching World* (Scottdale, Pa.: Herald Press, 1992), 26.

33. On this, see, e.g., Paul Peachey, ""Social Background and Social Philosophy of the Swiss Anabaptists, 1525-1540," *Mennonite Quarterly Review* 28:2 (April 1954), 120.

34. Walter Klaassen, *Anabaptism: Neither Catholic nor Protestant* (Waterloo, Ont.: Conrad Press, 1973), 60-63.

35. Leo Driedger, *Mennonite Identity in Conflict* (Lewiston, N.Y.: Edwin Mellen, 1988), 15. See also Harold S. Bender, "Church and State in Mennonite History," *Mennonite Quarterly Review* 13:2 (April 1939), especially 87-91.

36. C. Henry Smith gives a description of French Mennonites that is useful in this context. French Mennonite farmers had greater prosperity and better reputations among French noblemen than did their peers. "Frequent complaints were lodged against them with the ruling authorities, and demands made that they be driven from their holdings." These charges, says Smith, were usually economic, not religious or political. "In 1731 the French peasants in one local Mennonite community complained that the Mennonites monopolized all the work of the community, and by using up the wood in the local forests for their cheesemaking, greatly raised the cost of living for all. Later it was charged that by taking care of their own poor and orphans, settling their own disputes among themselves without going to law, and helping one another in time of need, they separated themselves from the rest of society and thus formed a dangerous self-governing local unit—a state within a state. See

C. Henry Smith, *Smith's Story of the Mennonites*, 5th. ed., revised and enlarged by Cornelius Krahn (Newton, Kan.: Faith and Life Press, 1981), 95.

37. John H. Yoder, editor and translator, *The Legacy of Michael Sattler* (Scottdale, Pa.: Herald Press, 1973), 39-40.

38. This is a distillation of Marpeck's "Defence," which is excerpted in Walter Klaassen, editor, *Anabaptism in Outline: Selected Primary Sources* (Scottdale, Pa.: Herald Press, 1981), 263.

39. William Klassen and Walter Klaassen, translators and editors, *The Writings of Pilgram Marpeck* (Scottdale, Pa.: Herald Press, 1978), 558.

40. On this, see C. Arnold Snyder, *Anabaptist History and Theology: An Introduction* (Kitchener, Ont.: Pandora Press, 1995), 189-190. For an overview of Marpeck's contributions to Anabaptism and his professional life, see, e.g., Cornelius J. Dyck, *An Introduction to Mennonite History*, 3rd. ed. (Scottdale, Pa., 1993), 81-95.

41. Peter Riedemann, *Peter Riedemann's Hutterite Confession of Faith*, translated and ed. John J. Friesen (Waterloo, Ont.: Herald Press, 1999), 131-133. Later, on p. 226, Riedemann writes, "Neither Christ's words nor Paul's words were intended to permit rulers to carry out every whim. Instead, they speak of those powers which God has assigned to rulers, such as compulsory labor, revenue, duties, and so on, for the purpose of allowing them to carry out their offices. Since Christ has not done away with this office, which exists for the unjust, its appointed service must remain. If the rulers are evil, the punishment of the people is even greater."

42. H. Wayne Pipkin and John H. Yoder, translators and editors, *Balthasar Hubmaier: Theologian of Anabaptism* (Scottdale, Pa.: Herald Press, 1989), 15.

43. In *The Anabaptist Vision* (Scottdale, Pa.: Herald Press, 1944), 41-42, Harold S. Bender writes that "not all the Anabaptists were completely nonresistant." Bender gives as his example Hubmaier, who led a group in Moravia that "agreed to carry the sword against the Turk and pay special war taxes for this purpose." Hubmaier's group, known as the "Schwertler," became extinct in short order, says Bender, adding that "it is obvious that Hubmaier and the 'Schwertler' represent a transient aberration from original and authentic Anabaptism."

44. H. Wayne Pipkin and John H. Yoder, *Balthasar Hubmaier*,

loc. cit., 500.

45. H. Wayne Pipkin and John H. Yoder, *Balthasar Hubmaier*, loc. cit., 503. As Pipkin and Yoder write (p. 493) in their introduction to Hubmaier's piece "On the Sword," from which this quote is taken, "Clearly [Hubmaier] did not have the negative understanding of civil government which many other Anabaptists had." Hubmaier also had a rather different view of vocation than that of many of his Anabaptist peers. He goes on to say (p. 521), in a discussion of Paul's Romans 13 passage, "If now the government did not have the authority to kill, why should the sword then hang at its side? It would then bear it in vain, which Paul cannot bear. He also explicitly adds that the authority is the servant of God. Where are now those who say a Christian cannot use the sword? For if a Christian could not be a servant of God, could not fulfill the mandate of God without sinning, then God would not be good. He would have made an order which a Christian could not fulfill without sin. That is a blasphemy."

46. C. Arnold Snyder suggests, in *Anabaptist History*, loc. cit., 192, that Hubmaier's arguments in "On the Sword" are "directed against Schleitheim's strict ethic of 'doing what Jesus did.'" However, Hubmaier, from his Nikolsburg context, makes no reference to the Schleitheim document, and may well have been unaware of it, as Yoder and Pipkin say. He clearly was aware of the Schleitheim themes, however, which suggests they were circulating among the various Anabaptist groups. Pipkin and Yoder note, p. 493, that nonpacifist views lost ground among the Zurich-based Anabaptists after the Schleitheim Confession, and in territories under Austrian rule after Hubmaier was killed in 1528. The Anabaptist debate about pacifism continued in the Netherlands until close to 1540.

47. C. Arnold Snyder, *Anabaptist History*, loc. cit., 227.

48. Zwingli and most other Reformers also agreed with this critique of interest. Zwingli says, in a 1523 sermon, "Interest is not godly, because God requires of us to lend or to sell on credit without expecting anything in return (Luke 6:25)." See Leland Harder, editor, *The Sources of Swiss Anabaptism: The Grebel Letters and Related Documents* (Scottdale, Pa.: Herald Press, 1985), 215.

49. On this, see C. Arnold Snyder, *Anabaptist History*, loc. cit., 226.

50. Also known as Sirach, from the full title, Ecclesiasticus, or

the Wisdom of Jesus Son of Sirach. Peter Riedemann quotes this same apocryphal passage in *Peter Riedemann's*, loc. cit., 149.

51. Menno Simons, "True Christian Faith," in J. C. Wenger, editor, and Leonard Verduin, translator, *The Complete Writings of Menno Simons, c. 1496-1561* (Scottdale, Pa.: Herald Press, 1956), 369.

52. Menno Simons, "True Christian Faith," loc. cit., 368.

53. Peter Riedemann, *Peter Riedemann's*, loc. cit., 149.

54. Peter Riedemann, *Peter Riedemann's*, loc. cit., 138.

55. Peter Riedemann, *Peter Riedemann's*, loc. cit., 149.

56. Harold S. Bender, "The Discipline Adopted by the Strasburg Conference of 1568," *Mennonite Quarterly Review* 1 (January 1927), 65. Cited in C. Arnold Snyder, *Anabaptist History*, loc. cit., 251-252.

57. C. Arnold Snyder, *Anabaptist History*, loc. cit., 248. For examples of this posture and tension in nineteenth-century U.S.-America, see Theron F. Schlabach, *Peace, Faith, Nation: Mennonites and Amish in Nineteenth-Century America* (Scottdale, Pa.: Herald Press, 1988), 58-59, 278ff. Snyder's statement contrasts significantly with a mid-twentieth-century statement by a study committee of General Conference Mennonites, who write: "We believe many persons are called to business as a vocation and as such are the servants of God and of the people. Therefore, we urge young people to enter its portals through which they might witness to the Light which was in Christ Jesus our Lord." The committee acknowledges, though, concern that the "intricate and complex maze of relationships which emerge" in business often tend to make Christians neglect their faith or dampen their witness on ethical issues. See Calvin Redekop, Victor A. Krahn, and Samuel J. Steiner, editors, *Anabaptist/Mennonite*, loc. cit., 400. The summary statement was sponsored by Western District General Conference and the Board of Christian Service of the General Conference Mennonite Church in Hillsboro, Kansas, 1955.

58. See See www.businessasacalling.org. The conference included papers on such topics as "Dare to Dream: The Risky Business of Believing Big for the Kingdom," "The Risky Business of Releasing God's Brilliance in Your Life," and "The Greatest Risk of All—Not Cultivating Our Faith in God." For a general overview of Mennonite perspectives on business, see also Calvin W. Redekop, "Business," in Cornelius J. Dyck and

Dennis D. Martin, editors, *Mennonite Encyclopedia*, Vol. V, loc. cit., 113-116.

59. Wally Kroeker, "The Wealthy in the Land," *The Mennonite* (19 April 2005), 12.

60. Wally Kroeker, "The Wealthy in the Land," loc. cit., 13. In reference to the "building bigger barns" story from Luke 12, Kroeker cites James Halteman, a Mennonite economist teaching at Wheaton (Ill.) College, as saying, "The contemporary farm, factory, or office building may well function, not as a store of existing resources, but rather as a vehicle for the production of future resources in greater and greater quantities." In another book, Sider writes, in the context of a discussion about Christian politicians and business leaders, the world would be transformed if a few thousand Christians would make this simple covenant with God: "I promise to submit every political act and every economic decision to your Lordship." See Ronald J. Sider, *Genuine Christianity: Essentials for Living Your Faith* (Grand Rapids: Zondervan, 1996), 133.

61. C. Arnold Snyder writes in *Anabaptist History*, loc. cit., 390-391, that perhaps we are witnessing the definitive "protestantization" of the Anabaptist remnant, "in which social and economic activity will be divorced fundamentally from spirituality. Or perhaps, given the way in which our church institutions covet and encourage large donations from our wealthier members, we are witnessing a return to the late medieval Catholic system, in which the 'churchly' use of one's wealth is valued as a positive aid to salvation. Or perhaps we are seeking the emergence of a 'two track' system in which those who are specially called to do the work of missions, evangelism, relief, and peace witness (much like religious in the Catholic system), are supported by the financial largesse of the 'less religious' laity who remain fully immersed in 'the world.'" Snyder thinks these developments probably are not a good thing. The early Anabaptists and the spiritual Christian stream that preceded them "had it right: the Christian life in this world, grows out of, and is an integral expression of, the new life in Christ; where there is true love of God, there must needs be a radical love of neighbour. What kind of 'discipleship' is left when the economic dimensions of the love of neighbor are passed over in polite silence?"

62. Calvin Redekop, Victor A. Krahn, and Samuel J. Steiner,

Anabaptist/Mennonite Faith and Economics (Lanham, Md.: University Press of America, 1994). Extremely helpful in this volume, in terms of tracking down sources, are Calvin Redekop's "Mennonites and Economics: Concluding Analysis," 373-382, and the appendix titled "Anabaptist/Mennonite Statement on Economic Matters," 383-403, the latter of which identifies a host of Anabaptist statements about economics from the sixteenth through the twentieth centuries.

63. C. Arnold Snyder, "Anabaptist Spirituality and Economics," in Calvin Redekop, Victor A. Krahn, and Samuel J. Steiner, *Anabaptist/Mennonite Faith*, loc. cit., 11.

64. J. L. Burkholder, "The Economic Problem for Mennonites," in Calvin Redekop, Victor A. Krahn, and Samuel J. Steiner, *Anabaptist/Mennonite Faith*, loc. cit., 368. For Burkholder's autobiographical reflections, which inform his particular perspective, see "The Limits of Perfection: Autobiographical Reflections," in Rodney J. Sawatsky and Scott Holland, editors, *The Limits of Perfection* (Waterloo, Ont.: Institute of Mennonite Studies, 1993), 1-54.

65. Paul Peachey, "Social Background," loc. cit., 104-105. This is a markedly detailed examination of the Swiss Anabaptists, with specific people named and numbered as craftspeople, clergy, lay intellectuals, nobility, tradespeople, and peasants.

66. Claus-Peter Clasen, *Anabaptism: A Social History, 1525-1618* (Ithaca: Cornell University Press, 1972), 318-322. Clasen's book is the best source regarding sixteenth- and early seventeenth-century Anabaptist occupations, and includes a list of numbers and occupations of "known Anabaptist intellectuals" and "known Anabaptist craftsmen" on pp. 432-436.

67. Paul Peachey, "Social Background," loc. cit., 105.

68. Claus-Peter Clasen, *Anabaptism*, loc. cit., 306.

69. As noted elsewhere, developments among the Dutch and North German Mennonites need to be treated separately. On this, see, e.g., Richard MacMaster, *Land, Piety, Peoplehood: The Establishment of Mennonite Communities in America, 1683-1790* (Scottdale, Pa.: Herald Press, 1985), 24ff.; James C. Juhnke, *Vision, Doctrine, War: Mennonite Identity and Organization in America, 1890-1930* (Scottdale, Pa.: Herald Press, 1989), 33-35.

70. Cornelius J. Dyck, *An Introduction to Mennonite History*, 3rd. ed. (Scottdale, Pa.: Herald Press, 1993), 407.

71. This term is used by J. Winfield Fretz in *The Waterloo*

Mennonites (Waterloo, Ont.: Wilfrid Laurier Press, 1989), 181.

72. Richard MacMaster, *Land, Piety*, loc. cit., 39. C. Henry Smith writes, in *Smith's Story*, p. 361, that these Germantown settlers were "not given much to agriculture."

73. Richard MacMaster, *Land Piety*, loc. cit., 85.

74. Richard MacMaster, *Land, Piety*, loc. cit., 101-102. MacMaster writes that "in 1756 in Perkiomen and Skippack Townships, Mennonites monopolized the cloth industry, providing the community with nine of ten weavers, the man who ran the fulling mill to bleach the cloth, and the dyer. Mennonites also owned the only two tanneries in the Skippack-Perkiomen region; and a Mennonite worked with leather as one of the cordwainers. Another founded one of the gristmills, and the locksmith was of Mennonite background." By the late eighteenth century, the expanding occupations of Mennonites included brewers and distillers, as was true in Europe as well. See MacMaster, p. 130, on this.

75. Richard MacMaster, *Land, Piety*, loc. cit., 140. Mennonites also did not avoid local officeholding, as is clear from MacMaster's text. See, e.g., his account on p. 198 of several Mennonites in Germantown in the late eighteenth century who were ministers and businesspeople as well as community leaders in both official and unofficial ways.

76. Donald B. Kraybill and Phyllis Pellman Good, editors, *The Perils of Professionalism: Essays on Christian Faith and Professionalism* (Scottdale, Pa.: Herald Press, 1982), 8.

77. Personal correspondence, David Schrock-Shenk to Keith Graber Miller, 13 October 2005. I am grateful to David, in his critique of an earlier draft of this book, for pushing me to tease out more clearly this reality.

78. David Schrock-Shenk noted that several years ago the Immigration and Naturalization Service conducted a pre-Thanksgiving Day raid on a chicken farm in one U.S. Mennonite mecca. A number of the undocumented immigrant laborers were regular attenders or members of a Mennonite fellowship. One of the plant's owners also was a member of a different Mennonite church. Personal correspondence, David Schrock-Shenk to Keith Graber Miller, 13 October 2005.

79. James C. Juhnke, *Vision, Doctrine*, loc. cit., 172, says that Bethel College alone trained 1,799 teachers between 1893 and 1953, more than five times the 333 students who went into

either ministry or mission fields.

80. On Mennonites' entry into *mental health* fields, see, e.g., Paul Toews, *Mennonites in American Society, 1930-1970* (Scottdale, Pa.: Herald Press, 1996), 165-169; Vernon H. Neufeld, editor, *If We Can Love: The Mennonite Mental Health Story* (Newton, Kan.: Faith and Life Press, 1983); and Albert N. Keim, *The CPS Story: An Illustrated History of Civilian Public Service* (Intercourse, Pa.: Good Books, 1990).

81. Paul Toews, *Mennonites*, loc. cit., 213.

82. Julia Kasdorf, *The Body and the Book*, loc. cit., 40-41. The phrase "liars and rascals" is from Hildi Froese Tiessen's book *Liars and Rascals* (Waterloo, Ont.: University of Waterloo Press, 1989), xii.

83. Ernst Correll, "The Sociological and Economic Significance of the Mennonites as a Culture Group in History," *Mennonite Quarterly Review* 16:3 (July 1942), 164. Emphasis in original. He cites as an example of this decline, on p. 165, the Western European urbanized Mennonites. He notes earlier than an exception to the rural, handicraft-driven Mennonites were "certain portions of the Dutch Doopsezinde groups" and the "North German movement" that were "more closely and more generally tied to a relatively advanced merchant civilization." While Dutch Mennonites represented a substantial percentage of the sixteenth- and seventeenth-century Mennonite population in Europe, they were quite different from their faith siblings in south Germany, France, Switzerland, Austria, Bohemia, Prussia, and later Russia and North America. See Calvin Redekop, "Mennonites, Creation," loc. cit. Correll's comments about the Dutch and North German Mennonites represents well a critique mid-twentieth-century Old Mennonites shared of their Dutch counterparts. Correll finishes his article, p. 166, with the flourish, "May God bless you in your endeavors to safeguard a high and saintly heritage!" The entire issue of *MQR* is fascinating with its attention to small-community values believed to be essential for maintaining the Ana-baptist/Mennonite heritage. For a counter-perspective to Correll's about the effects of progressive urbanization, see Mary S. Sprunger, "Dutch Mennonites and the Golden Age Economy: The Problem of Social Disparity in the Church," in Calvin Redekop, Victor A. Krahn, and Samuel J. Steiner, *Anabaptst/Mennonite Faith and Economics*, loc. cit., 18-40.

Sprunger begins by citing the aphorism attributed to a twentieth-century Dutch Mennonite pastor: "After the devil failed in his attempt to destroy Dutch Anabaptism by means of persecution, he almost succeeded when he changed his tactics and made them rich." Sprunger says this view of Dutch Mennonite prosperity and the resulting demise of Anabaptist ideals is "largely uninformed."

84. In the sociological study, eight percent of U.S. Mennonites also said they were in each of the following: precision production, craft, and repair; operators, fabricators, and laborers; and service. Three percent said they were students. On this recent data, see Conrad L. Kanagy, *Road Signs for the Journey: A Profile of Mennonite Church USA* (Scottdale, Pa.: Herald Press, 2007), 58-59. Earlier studies done at 17-year intervals included both U.S. and Canadian Mennonites of various sorts. See J. Howard Kauffman and Leo Driedger, *The Mennonite Mosaic: Identity and Modernization* (Scottdale, Pa.: Herald Press, 1991); and J. Howard Kauffman and Leland Harder, *Anabaptists Four Centuries Later: A Profile of Five Mennonite and Brethren in Christ Denominations* (Scottdale, Pa.: Herald Press, 1975). For reports on earlier studies of men's occupations, see also Toews, *Mennonites*, loc. cit., 188-191.

85. John W. Eby, "Professionalism: Faith, Ethics, and Christian Identity," in *Professionalism*, loc. cit., 27.

86. On the Mennonite Community movement, see J. Winfield Fretz, "Community," *Mennonite Encyclopedia I*, ed. Harold S. Bender et. al. (Newton, Kan.: Mennonite Publication Office, 1955),656-658. See also various writings by Hershberger in the 1940s and 1950s as well as the special April 1945 issue of *Mennonite Quarterly Review* dedicated to Mennonite Community. Another description of the movement can be found in Paul Toews, *Mennonites,* loc. cit., 195-197. Guy F. Hershberger and J. Winfield Fretz were leaders behind the community movement, but other Mennonite Community Association members included Clayton Keener, John L. Yoder, A. J. Metzler, Harold S. Bender, Ivan Miller, and Paul Erb. In an unpublished, mimeographed paper by Simon Gingerich, "Occupations of Mennonite Men" (Mennonite Historical Library, 1950), 57, Gingerich writes: "The Industrial Relations Committee of The Mennonite General Conference, *The Mennonite Community*, and the Mennonite church schools

should continue their emphasis upon the values of rural life and seek by wholesome propaganda to prevent any unnecessary and ill advised movements of people from agriculture to occupations where the environmental factors militate against spiritual growth."

87. E. E. Miller, "Opportunities in the Professions," *Christian Living* (September 1956), 16-17, 40-41. This use of the parable of the talents comes up several times in Mennonite writings of the last several decades. See also Melvin Lehman, "Within or Outside the System: The Concept of Paradox and Mennonite Identity," in *Conflict,* loc. cit., 57; and June A. Yoder, "What Mennonites Believe about Vocations" (Scottdale, Pa.: Mennonite Publishing House, 1979), 7. Available in photocopied form in Mennonite Historical Library. However, John H. Yoder and others have criticized this as a misapplication of "talents," which is a reference to money in its biblical context rather than our gifts and abilities.

88. Gordon D. Kaufman, "Mennonites and Professionalism," in Arden Shank and Richard Mojonnier, editors, mimeographed text *Professionalism: Faith, Ethics, and Christian Identity* (Philadelphia, Pa.; Eastern Area Mennonite Student Services), 14. Available in Mennonite Historical Library.

89. Gordon D. Kaufman, "Mennonites and Professionalism," loc. cit., 20-23.

90. Paul Peachey, "Profession, Person, and the Common Good," in Shank, Burkholder, and Peachey, *Conflict,* loc. cit., 10.

91. Donald B. Kraybill and Phyllis Pellman Good, *The Perils,* loc. cit., 10.

92. Phyllis Pellman Good, "Mennonite Professionals Feel Tug of the World," *The Philadelphia Inquirer* (27 September 1982), A-9.

93. Calvin Redekop and Urie A. Bender, *Who Am I? What Am I? Searching for Meaning in Your Work,* loc. cit.. The book was withdrawn by Academie Books, a subsidiary of Zondervan, almost the day it was published, so it received little promotion or distribution. In personal e-mail correspondence (Calvin Redekop to Keith Graber Miller, 12 October 2005), the co-author suggested that the book may not have been sufficiently evangelical for the press. Unfortunately, the book has not been used within Mennonite churches, where it would have been an excellent resource.

94. The books include Rodney J. Sawatsky, *Authority and Identity* (North Newton, Kan.: Bethel College, 1987); Leo Driedger, *Mennonite Identity in Conflict* (Lewiston, New York: Edwin Mellen Press, 1988); Calvin Wall Redekop and Samuel J. Steiner, *Mennonite Identity: Historical and Contemporary Perspectives* (New York, New York: University Press of America, 1988); Harry Loewen, editor, *Why I Am a Mennonite: Essays on Mennonite Identity* (Scottdale, Pa.: Herald Press, 1988); Calvin Redekop, *Mennonite Identity* (Baltimore: The Johns Hopkins University Press, 1989); and Leo Driedger and Leland Harder, editors, *Anabaptist-Mennonite Identities in Ferment* (Elkhart, Indiana: Institute of Mennonite Studies, 1990).

95. Leo Driedger and J. Howard Kauffman, *The Mennonite Mosaic: Identity and Modernization* (Scottdale, Pa.: Herald Press, 1991).

96. For example, see Leland Harder, *The Pastor-People Partnership: The Call and Recall of Pastors from a Believers' Church Perspective* (Elkhart, Indiana, and Bluffton, Ohio: Institute of Mennonite Studies and Central District Conference Ministerial Committee, 1983); Paul M. Zehr and Jim Egli, *Alternative Models of Mennonite Pastoral Formation* (Elkhart, Indiana: Institute of Mennonite Studies, 1992); and John A. Esau, editor, *Understanding Ministerial Leadership: Essays Contributing to a Developing Theology of Ministry* (Elkhart, Indiana: Institute of Mennonite Studies, 1995).

97. For example, see Calvin Redekop, Victor A. Krahn, and Samuel J. Steiner, editors, *Anabaptist/Mennonite Faith and Economics*, loc. cit; and Calvin W. Redekop and Benjamin W. Redekop, *Entrepreneurs in the Faith Community: Profiles of Mennonites in Business* (Scottdale, Pa.: Herald Press, 1996).

98. Benjamin Redekop and Calvin W. Redekop, editors, *Power, Authority, and the Anabaptist Tradition* (Baltimore: The Johns Hopkins University Press, 2001).

99. The interviewer mentioned here was David Schrock-Shenk, who talked with Russian Mennonites in Canada for a Mennonite Central Committee project in the 1990s and recognized the power of what his interviewees brought with them to their new country. Personal interview with Schrock-Shenk, 12 August 2003. Much has been written about the Russian Mennonite experience. Among these sources is C. Henry Smith, *Smith's Story*, loc. cit., 249-356. For an accounting of tragic devel-

opments in Russia in relation to economic success and self-governing, see Jacob A. Loewen and Wesley J. Prieb, "The Abuse of Power Among Mennonites in South Russia, 1789-1919," in Benjamin W. Redekop and Calvin W. Redekop, editors, *Power, Authority, and the Anabaptist Tradition*, loc. cit.

100. On this, see also the poignant account, in Sue Monk Kidd's *The Secret Life of Bees* (New York: Penguin Books, 2002), of a conversation between the primary character Lily, a white southern girl, and her African-American friend Zach. The conversation takes place in the summer of 1964 in the Deep South. Zach speaks about not having much of a future because he is "a negro." When he tells Lily he really wants to be a lawyer, she expresses surprise since she's never heard of a "negro lawyer." "You've got to hear of things before you can imagine them," she says. Zach responds, in contrast, "You gotta imagine what's never been."

101. On Anabaptist anticlericalism, see A. James Reimer's review of several examinations of the theme in "Book Review," *Religious Studies Review* 29:3 (July 2003).

102. C. Arnold Snyder, *Anabaptist History*, loc. cit., 366-267, says the anticlericalism of the Anabaptists lasted throughout at least the sixteenth century, with clergy outside the Anabaptist communities described by Anabaptists as "ravening wolves in sheeps' clothing." Pastors in the sixteenth-century and later Anabaptist tradition continued to be lay ministers rather than salaried clergy, and were subject to discipline.

103. C. Arnold Snyder, *Anabaptist History*, loc. cit., 383, says that when sixteenth-century Anabaptists determined that the only true pastors were those who were chosen and commissioned by elders or the congregation, this essentially "rendered the priesthood of all believers functionally obsolete." Today, he writes, most Believers' Church members do not function as "priests," interpreting Scripture and carrying out other traditionally pastoral tasks.

104. Some recent Mennonite scholars have questioned the extent of the Anabaptist embrace of the concept of the "priesthood of all believers." Worth hearing is Marlin E. Miller's observation that in his search for Anabaptist and Mennonite sources on the "priesthood of all believers," he found only two pages, and those were from Menno Simons' *Complete Works*. Miller questions whether the use of this concept by Mennonites over

the last century wasn't a kind of anachronistic reading back into the sixteenth-century movement. The term was developed by Luther and used more on that side of the Reformation than by the Radical Reformers. See Richard A. Kauffman and Gayle Gerber Koontz, editors, *Theology for the Church: Writings by Marlin E. Miller* (Elkhart, Indiana: Institute of Mennonite Studies, 1997), 123-124; and Marlin E. Miller, "Priesthood of all Believers," in Cornelius J. Dyck and Dennis D. Martin, *Mennonite Encyclopedia*, Vol. V, loc. cit., 721-722.

105. Public execution of Anabaptists, who continued to be politically suspect, lasted from 1525 to 1614, and others later died in prison. Early Anabaptist martyrdoms, writes sociologist Paul Peachey, were a "severe blow to the spiritual development of the new movement .... The genius of spiritual renewal represented by Anabaptism was thus lost at a time when the influence was sorely needed in the cities. Perhaps even more tragic was the effect upon the movement itself, for the loss of contact with the urban population prevented the replacement of competent leadership from the clergy and other educated circles. The result was crippling and in time led to spiritual stagnation." See Paul Peachey, "Social Background," loc. cit., 115.

106. On this, see John Oyer and Keith Graber Miller, "Worshiping with the Early Anabaptists," in *What Mennonites Are Thinking 1998*, ed. Merle Good and Phyllis Pellman Good (Intercourse, Pa.: Good Books, 1998), 123.

107. Peter Riedemann, *Peter Riedemann's*, loc. cit., 113.

108. John H. Yoder, editor and translator, *The Legacy*, loc. cit., 39. Perhaps not surprisingly, Yoder includes a footnote clarifying the word` he translates as "ordained." He writes, p. 52: "Perhaps 'installed' would be less open to the sacramental misunderstanding. *Verordnet* has no sacramental meaning."

109. Cornelius J. Dyck, William E. Keeney, and Alvin J. Beachy, translators and editors, *The Writings of Dirk Philips, 1504-1568* (Scottdale, Pa.: Herald Press, 1992), 201-203.

110. Peter Riedemann, *Peter Riedemann's*, loc. cit., 112.

111. James C. Juhnke, *Vision, Doctrine, War: Mennonite Identity and Organization in America, 1890-1930* (Scottdale, Pa.: Herald Press, 1989), 63. The lot, says Juhnke, included nomination of candidates by the congregation, with each member allowed to submit one name. "The nominees were examined for their willingness to obey God and the church, a promise implicit in their

baptism. New ministers, deacons, and bishops were finally selected and ordained to office in a single solemn ceremony in which the candidates (as many as a dozen in a single lot) each chose a book from a set of songbooks on the singers' table. One book contained a slip with a certain Bible verse indicating that the holder had been chosen: 'The lot is cast into the lap; but the whole disposing thereof is of the Lord' (Proverbs 16:33)." On p. 64, Juhnke writes that "paradoxically, to have influence and a kind of power, ministers and bishops had to master the rituals of powerlessness, nonresistance, and humility."

112. Ervin R. Stutzman, "Preacher's Calling: For John Ruth, It Meant a Lot," in Reuben Z. Miller and Joseph S Miller, editors, *The Measure of My Days* (Telford, Pa.: Cascadia Publishing House, 2004), 147. In his account, Stutzman evidences both the strengths and the tragic weaknesses related to the lot, drawing extensively on John Ruth's work on Franconia Mennonites. Stutzman concludes by suggesting that the following spiritual disciplines for selecting ministers should be received from the old tradition: "an emphasis on both inner call and outer call; a definition of vocation as Christ's call to discipleship; a close link between baptism and call to ministry; a definition of occupation as the concrete application of Christian vocation; an opportunity for congregational members to name potential pastoral leaders; a congregational process of discernment to select the best suited candidates; an openness to transcendence and mystery in the choice of a candidate."

113. Everett J. Thomas, editor, *A Mennonite Polity for Ministerial Leadership* (Newton, Kan.: Faith and Life Press, 1996) 17-18. The polity manual was co-sponsored by Mennonite Board of Congregational Ministries in Elkhart, Ind., and the Ministerial Leadership Services and General Board of the General Conference Mennonite Church, Newton, Kan. The text was pulled together in the years leading up to the 2002 "integration" of the Mennonite Church and the General Conference Mennonite Church.

114. On this, see Everett J. Thomas, editor, *A Mennonite Polity*, loc. cit., 93-105.

115. General Conference Mennonite churches began this shift earlier in the twentieth century than did Old Mennonites (Mennonite Church) congregations. See, e.g., Leland Harder, *The Pastor-People Partnership: The Call and Recall of Pastors from a*

Believers' Church Perspective (Elkhart, Ind.: Institute of Mennonite Studies, 1983), 12-13.

116. John A. Esau, *Understanding Ministerial Leadership: Essays Contributing to a Developing Theology of Ministry* (Elkhart, Ind.: Institute of Mennonite Studies, 1995), xi-xii. At the time of the book's publication Esau was Director of Ministerial Leadership Services for the General Conference Mennonite Church. Esau writes, on p. 43, "If we see the call to ministry as divine and not only human, then ordination is not only to a function but also to an office."

117. See also John A. Esau, "Ordination," in Cornelius J. Dyck and Dennis D. Martin, *Mennonite Encyclopedia*, Vol. V, loc. cit., 660-662.

118. See, e.g., Dorothy Yoder Nyce and Lynda Nyce, "Power and Authority in Mennonite Ecclesiology: A Feminist Perspective," in Benjamin Redekop and Calvin Wall Redekop, *Power, Authority,* loc. cit., 161. Yoder Nyce and Nyce also speak about the denial of power in Mennonite leadership roles, quoting a Mennonite agency CEO as saying, when asked about the extent of his power, "Oh, I don't think of myself as having power." "Such a denial," say Yoder Nyce and Nyce, "should alert those who might be under his influence."

119. Both John Howard Yoder and Virgil Vogt were participants in the *Concern* movement of the 1950s and early 1960s. J. Lawrence Burkholder writes, "Concern Pamphlets Movement," *Mennonite Encyclopedia V,* loc. cit., 178, regarding *Concern* participants, "With respect to the nature of the church, articles appeared from the outset that expressed disillusionment with the Mennonite church for its alleged conformity to denominational patterns of organization and religious life. Especially offensive was the apparent identification of the church with vertical structures, as represented by conferences, ministerial boards, and institutions .... What emerged was a vision of the church according to which spirit supersedes structure, essence transcends form, and the simple resists the complex. The church is not to be understood as a building or as an institution but as an intimate fellowship of believers within which interaction includes mutual support, Bible study, edification, and discipline. The church is defined as 'where two or three are gathered together in the presence of Jesus.'"

120. John H. Yoder, *Body Politics,* loc. cit., 56.

121. John H. Yoder, *Body Politics*, loc. cit., 60. The context for this discussion is that of gender debates about allowing women into ministry. Yoder says Paul's vision is larger than allowing a few more especially gifted women to share with a few men the rare roles of domination. This might be a good form of "affirmative action," but its hardly "a profound vision of renewal."

122. Everett J. Thomas, editor, *A Mennonite Polity*, loc. cit., 27.

123. John Howard Yoder, *The Politics of Jesus: Behold the Man! Our Victorious Lamb*, 2nd. ed. (Grand Rapids, Mich.: William B. Eerdmans Publishing Company, 1994), 22.

124. Cited in Stutzman, "Preacher's Calling," 138.

125. On this, see Schuurman, *Vocation*, 17ff.

126. On this, see, e.g., Duane K. Friesen, "On Doing Social Ethics: A Personal Response," in Rodney J. Sawatsky and Scott Holland, *The Limits of Perfection*, loc. cit., 122-129.

127. The quoted material here is from Schuurman, *Vocation*, 47, though Schuurman completes the quote by saying "refracts God's general call into the variety of particular callings in the life of an individual or community."

128. See also Karl Barth, *Church Dogmatics* 3/4, edited and translated by G.W. Bromiley (Edinburgh: T & T Clark, 1961), on this. Barth had a significant influence on Mennonite theologian John H. Yoder.

129. In his article "God's Double Agents," *The Mennonite* (19 April 2005), 9-10, Wally Kroeker suggests commissioning people for their day-to-day work, planning a series of "workplace testimonies" for churches, having pastors visit members at their work settings, or having people coming to a special Sunday service in their work garb. On this, see also Ben Sprunger, Carol J. Suter, and Wally Kroeker, editors, *Faith Dilemmas for Marketplace Christians* (Scottdale, Pa.: Herald Press, 1997), 17.

130. Sociologist Thomas J. Meyers addresses these issues in "Response," in Driedger and Harder, *Anabaptist-Mennonite Identities*, loc. cit., 87.

131. Yoder, *Body Politics*, loc. cit., 27.

132. Eby, "Professionalism," 35. On such subversion, see also Redekop and Bender, *Who Am I?*, loc. cit., 131-144.

133. Yoder, *The Royal Priesthood*, loc. cit., 81.

134. Yoder, *The Royal Priesthood*, loc. cit., 81.

135. I am grateful to David Schrock-Shenk for suggesting, in his response to an earlier draft of this book, the "conscientious

objection" language in this context. Personal correspondence, David Schrock-Shenk to Keith Graber Miller, 13 October 2005.

136. It would be fascinating to do a study of recent Mennonite patterns of *leaving* work. At what point have Mennonites chosen to leave the "stations" or "offices" for which they have prepared themselves, and why? See, e.g., Romans 12:2: "Do not be conformed to this world, but be transformed by the renewing of your minds, so that you may discern what is the will of God—what is good and acceptable and perfect." On the specific question of, e.g., the appropriateness of Mennonites being police, see Andy Alexis-Baker, "The Gospel or a Glock? Mennonites and the Police," *Conrad Grebel Review* 25:2 (Spring 2007), 23-49.

137. Yoder, *Body Politics*, loc. cit., 60.

138. Mary Lehman Yoder, one of three pastors at Assembly Mennonite Church in Goshen, Ind., called my attention to this useful term.

139. On calling Mennonite young people to ministry, see Rich Preheim, "Wherever Is Heard an Encouraging Word? Study: Church Falls Short in Promoting Pastorate," *The Mennonite* (18 January 2000), 8. Preheim's article is about "The Samuel Project," a two-phase study of Mennonite congregations and the broader church done by Michael D. Wiese of Anderson University. See Michael D. Wiese, "The Samuel Project: A Study of Pastoral Development in the Church (General Conference and Mennonite Church in the United States and Canada)," photocopied report, July 1999, available from the Congregational and Ministerial Leadership office, Mennonite Church U.S.A. See also Michael Wiese, "The Samuel II Project," photocopied report, 11 December 2000, available from the Congregational and Ministerial Leadership office, Mennonite Church U.S.A.

140. Robb Davis, "Faith and Malaria," Goshen College Chapel, 23 September 2005. Although Davis worked from a printed text, the comments here are from my notes from the presentation. A much earlier, but similarly worthwhile presentation, was J.R. Burkholder's "An Unlikely Oration on Church Occupation," an unpublished, mimeographed sermon, 5 March 1969, p. 4. Available from the author. Burkholder argues that Mennonite colleges might need to spend less time on developing technical skills to deal with the world's problems such as poverty, hunger, and violence, but more time on "what it means

to persuade." "Look at the problems that face American society; many of them are basically technical—medical care, hunger, urban decay, transportation tie-ups—these are all problems that are in principle solved, or solvable, IF there were only the will to do what needs to be done. There's no need for new scientific discoveries or break-throughs, there is only the need for persuasion to get the job done." On educational institutions, see also Albert J. Meyer, "Our Understanding of Christian Vocation and Its Implications for Education in the Church College," an unpublished, mimeographed paper (1962). Meyer's paper was one of five presented to a "theological workshop" that brought together teaching faculty from Eastern Mennonite College, Hesston College, Goshen, College, and Goshen Biblical Seminary.

141. One of the horrific realities is that our economic and governmental systems, in which most of us are deeply invested, often make such "faithfully made lives" impossible for the majority of the world's population to attain.

142. This story is from Mary Moschella's Harvard Divinity School baccalaureate address (8 June 1983), as told in Sharon Parks, *The Critical Years: Young Adults and the Search for Meaning, Faith, and Commitment* (San Francisco: HarperSanFrancisco, 1986), 129-131.

143. Personal interview with Esther and Ron Graber, 11 October 2009. Chester, the retirement consultant who came to their home, later became the Polish consul in Miami. Chester and his brother had gone to the docks in August 1946 to receive one of the horses Ron and his companions had brought.

144. Miroslav Volf, *Exclusion and Embrace* (Nashville: Abingdon Press, 1996).

SUBJECT INDEX

SCRIPTURE INDEX

THE AUTHOR

Keith Graber Miller, Ph.D., is professor of Bible, Religion, and Philosophy at Goshen (Ind.) College, teaching primarily in the areas of ethics, theology, religious history, and religion and sexuality. An ordained pastor in Mennonite Church USA, he previously served as a congregational and campus pastor, and worked briefly as a journalist just out of college.

Born in Kokomo, Indiana, Keith completed his B.A. at Franklin (Ind.) College, his M.Div. at Associated Mennonite Biblical Seminary, and his Ph.D. at Emory University. He is the author or editor of five previous books, including *Prophetic Peacemaking: Writings of John Richard Burkholder* (Institute of Mennonite Studies and Herald Press), winner of the 2012 Dale Brown Book Award.

Keith is a member and elder at Assembly Mennonite Church, Goshen, Indiana; the spouse of artist Ann Graber Miller, with whom he co-owns Found, an international art gallery in Goshen; and father of Niles, Mia, and Simon, who are working their way through middle school, high school, and college. He speaks broadly at youth conventions, college campuses, and in congregations on ethics, religion and politics, and sexuality.

CPSIA information can be obtained at www.ICGtesting.com
Printed in the USA
LVOW07s1714021113

359642LV00004B/31/P